T0351032

The Zero Trust Framework and Privileged Access Management (PAM)

This book is about the Zero Trust Framework. Essentially, this is a methodology where the IT/Network Infrastructure of a business is segmented into smaller islands, each having its own lines of defense. This is primarily achieved through the use of Multifactor Authentication (MFA), where at least three more authentication layers are used, preferably being different from one another.

Another key aspect of the Zero Trust Framework is known as Privileged Access Management (PAM). This is an area of Cybersecurity where the protection of superuser accounts, rights, and privileges must be protected at all costs from Cyberattackers. In this regard, this is where the Zero Trust Framework and PAM intertwine, especially in a Cloud-based platform, such as Microsoft Azure.

However, as it has been reviewed in one of our previous books, the use of passwords is now becoming a nemesis, not only for individuals but for businesses as well. It is hoped that by combining the Zero Trust Framework with PAM, password use can be eradicated altogether, thus giving rise to a passwordless society.

Ravindra Das is a technical writer in the field of Cybersecurity. He also does Cybersecurity consulting on the side, through his private practice, RaviDas.Tech, Inc. He also holds a Cybersecurity certification from the ISC(2) and other key certifications from Microsoft, CyberArk, and Barracuda Networks.

The Zero Trust Framework and Privileged Access Management (PAM)

Ravindra Das

CRC Press
Taylor & Francis Group
Boca Raton London New York

CRC Press is an imprint of the
Taylor & Francis Group, an **informa** business

Designed cover image: © Shutterstock

First edition published 2024
by CRC Press
2385 NW Executive Center Drive, Suite 320, Boca Raton FL 33431

and by CRC Press
4 Park Square, Milton Park, Abingdon, Oxon, OX14 4RN

CRC Press is an imprint of Taylor & Francis Group, LLC

© 2024 Ravindra Das

ISBN: 978-1-032-74257-1 (hbk)
ISBN: 978-1-032-74600-5 (pbk)
ISBN: 978-1-003-47002-1 (ebk)

DOI: 10.1201/9781003470021

Typeset in Caslon
by Apex CoVantage, LLC

This book is dedicated to my Lord and Savior, Jesus Christ, the Grand Designer of the Universe, and to my parents, Dr. Gopal Das and Mrs. Kunda Das.

This book is also dedicated to:
Richard and Gwynda Bowman
Barbara Dawson
Greg and Kelly Johnson
The Parkitny Family
Jaya Chandra
Ashis and Ila Das
My loving cats, Fifi and Bubu

Contents

Acknowledgment

I would like to thank Ms. Gabrielle Williams, my editor, who made this book a reality.

1

INTRODUCTION

The world of Cybersecurity is now a complex one. Gone are the days when it was all just about phishing attacks like in the late 1990s. Now it is a myriad of threat vectors, psychological tactics, and essentially digital warfare among nations and their peoples. Unfortunately, as time goes on, this is only going to get worse. This is best exemplified by the conflict between Russia and Ukraine. This war has been going on for almost a year now, with no end in sight.

True, there are the military machines of war present. But there is now a twist – Cyberattacks being launched against the Ukrainians by the Russians. Never has this happened before in the history of warfare. In fact, it is expected that even future wars will be fought mostly on the digital front, as there will be no further need for the physical armor to be present.

Even future terrorist attacks will not involve airplanes crashing into buildings like we saw during 9/11. Now, it will be a series of large-scale Cyberattacks aimed at the Critical Infrastructures of any one country. These will be simultaneous attacks aimed toward the oil and gas pipelines, water supplies, the food distribution system, the national power grid, and even the nuclear facilities of a country, literally bringing it down to its knees.

Even though the threat variants have become much more dangerous and covert and even stealthier, so have the advancements made in the various security technologies and tools that are designed to protect not only businesses but also individuals. For example, the tools of Artificial Intelligence and Machine Learning are now being used to speed and automate processes that would take days to achieve. Now, these tools are used to comb through large amounts of data to unearth any hidden trends that could prove to be useful for any IT Security team.

DOI: 10.1201/9781003470021-1

To some degree, they are also being used to predict what the future Cyber Threat landscape could potentially look like, as well as what the threat variants could be. However, it should be noted that these tools are only as good as the data that is being fed into them. In other words, garbage in and garbage out. Intelligence sharing has also greatly increased, between both the private and governmental sectors. This has proven to be of great benefit, as the FBI has been able to take some of the most notorious Ransomware groups and even retrieve the money that was paid as ransom to the hackers.

But, even despite all of this, it still seems like that it is not enough. The crux of the problem here is that businesses in Corporate America are simply way too reactive. The attitude seems to be like this: "If it has not hit me yet, the chances are that it will never happen". This is the main reason that people are so ignorant about security issues. The other piece of the puzzle that is often left to blame here in this regard is the cost of implementing security controls.

True, conducting a Risk Assessment can be a very exhaustive and time-constrained activity, but the truth of the matter is that security controls are now very affordable today, especially for the Small- and Medium-Sized Businesses (SMBs). Another problem here is that the primary tool that is used for authentication and authorization has been and continues to be the traditional password.

There have been many advances made in password security, especially that of the Password Manager. For example, it can create very long and complex passwords that are almost very difficult to break. It can even remind employees when they need to reset their passwords, or it can even do it automatically for them. It can also alert the employee if their password has been compromised in any way. Despite all of this, people are still afraid to use it just because this will mean a change in the routines things are done. By nature, humans are very resistant to change, and this is part of the reason why Cyberattackers can still carry the way they do. This is an issue that will be further addressed in the last chapter of this book.

Thus, the only way to guarantee that a business or an individual can be mitigated as much as possible from a security breach is to take extreme measures of all kinds. One such example of this is known as the "Zero Trust Framework". In this methodology, absolutely nobody or anything is to be trusted in both the external and internal environments. People simply cannot use their passwords anymore to gain access to the resources that they need to conduct their everyday job functions.

Instead, employees must be constantly verified all of the time, going through at least three or more layers of proving and confirming their identities. Also, the IT and Network Infrastructure of an organization is broken down into different layers or segments, to make sure that the Cyberattacker cannot break through any further. The thinking here is that if the Cyberattacker can break through the first lines of defenses, the chances that they can break through the other subsequent ones become almost nil.

This is a far cry from the traditional approaches, which were called the Perimeter Defense Model. With this kind of methodology, a business was surrounded by just one layer of defense, in a circle. Although this would have been heavily fortified, if the Cyberattacker were to break through, they would then literally have free reigns over all of the digital assets of the company.

In this regard, the Zero Trust Framework can totally supersede the Perimeter Defense Model, with all of the internal layers of security that it consists of. Although the Zero Trust Framework is, once again, viewed as an extreme, this is what is needed today to thwart Cyberattackers to the greatest degree possible.

Although this methodology has been around for quite some time (around ten years or so), not until now has it been formally adopted to varying degrees. But, for the most part, there has been a success rate with it, as it has been more difficult for the Cyberattacker to penetrate.

Thus, the primary goal of this book is to review the Zero Trust Framework and how it can be possibly deployed even at your organization, along with Privileged Access Management (PAM).

2
THE ZERO TRUST FRAMEWORK

The Origins of the Zero Trust Framework

In reality, the concept of the Zero Trust Framework is nothing new. In fact, it dates back more than a decade ago, all the way to 2010. John Kindervag developed the philosophy that nothing should be trusted at all, from within both the external and internal environments of a company or, for that matter, any type of entity. The motto here was to get rid all of the levels of trust, even how slight it may be. The driving philosophy was to "never trust, but always verify, no matter how many times it has to be done".

Although the concept of the Internet of Things (IoT) was not even heard back during those times, people trying to access connected devices could not be trusted, and everybody had to go through the same regimen of verification. John Kindervag even related this concept to Joseph Stalin with his famous quote, "I trust no one, not even myself". Eventually, he named his theory the Zero Trust Framework. Thus, as it will be elaborated more later in this chapter, the Zero Trust Framework is not a "one-size-fits-all" approach.

This means that whatever works for one entity regarding the Zero Trust Framework will not work for a different one. Rather, it is a methodology that has to be crafted and molded to the exact and unique security requirements of the company.

Probably the first true commercial application of the Zero Trust Framework came back when the U.S. Office of Personnel Management was hit by a Cyberattack. The House of Representatives mandated the use of the Zero Trust Framework methodology to safeguard not only their digital assets but also the rest of the U.S. Federal Government.

Other notable events in the history of the Zero Trust Framework which has led to its higher levels of adoption today follow.

DOI: 10.1201/9781003470021-2

In 2011

Google came out with its own version of the Zero Trust Framework, "BeyondCorp". The main trigger for this was the Cyberattack known as "Operation Aurora", which was launched in 2009. This was deemed to be an Advanced Persistent Threat (also known as "APT"). The premise behind this model was to do away with network segmentation altogether and rely upon the use of Multifactor Authentication (MFA) as the main source for both authentication and authorization. More information about Beyond Corp can be seen at www.beyondcorp.com/ In 2014, Google published a whitepaper about their proposed framework, which gave a rather big boost to the overall concept of the Zero Trust Framework. This is deemed to be an important piece of work, and it can be downloaded and viewed at this link: http://cyberresources.solutions/ZTF_Book/Beyond_Corp.pdf

In 2018

Forrester came up with their own model of the Zero Trust Framework, which was entitled the "Zero Trust eXtended Ecosystem". This methodology consisted of seven different layers, which are as follows:

- Workforce Security.
- Device Security.
- Workload.
- Network.
- Data Security.
- Visibility and Analytics.
- Automation and Orchestration.

Also, the National Institute of Standards and Technology came out with yet their version of the Zero Trust Framework, and this was released as Special Publication 800–207. Subsequently in 2020, this publication was updated.

In 2019

Gartner, in a manner similar to that of Forrester, also launched its version of the Zero Trust Framework, which was called the "Zero Trust

Network Access" (also known as the "ZTNA"). In return this also gave birth to a new Cyber concept (and even tool) called the "Secure Access Service Edge", also more commonly known as "SASE". The premise of this is that any processing and transactions of datasets occur close to the device that is requesting these services rather than having them done at the central database server.

In 2021

Another major catalyst for the adoption of the Zero Trust Framework was the COVID-19 pandemic. With everybody now working from home, businesses were seeking new ways to counter the new threat variants which persisted. In fact, according to a research report which was published by Microsoft entitled the "Zero Trust Adoption Report", an overwhelming 96% of the 1,200 respondents polled said that they favored the concepts of the overall concepts of the Zero Trust Framework.

From 2021 to Present

The Biden Administration has been the main trigger during this time frame, with the following events being the main drivers:

- Executive Order on Improving the Nation's Cybersecurity: This was signed in May 2021, with the main intention of enhancing the security posture of the U.S. Federal Government and the nation's Critical Infrastructure.
- The U.S. Office of Management and Budget (also known as the "OMB") further endorsed the adoption of the Zero Trust Framework.
- The Cybersecurity and Infrastructure Security Agency (also known as the "CISA") also came out with a different version of the Zero Trust Framework, and it was called the "Cloud Security Technical Reference Architecture and Zero Trust Maturity Model". This methodology focused more on Cloud-based security, especially focusing on data leakages, whether intentional or not.

- The Acting Director of the OMB (Shalanda D. Young) gave Federal Agencies until the end of the Fiscal Year of 2024 to deploy and implement certain controls to fulfill the following objectives of their version of the Zero Trust Framework:
  o Identity.
  o Devices.
  o Networks.
  o Applications and Data.
- The CISA came and published the second version of their Cloud Security/Zero Trust Framework Publication. It can be downloaded and viewed here: http://cyberresources.solutions/ ZTF_Book/CISA_Publication.pdf
- Okta conducted a major market research project which was entitled "The State of Zero Trust Security 2022". It was discovered that at least 72% of all of the Federal Agencies had some sort of Zero Trust plan in place or they were at least working on the first drafts of one.

(Source: www.techtarget.com/whatis/feature/History-
and-evolution-of-zero-trust-security)

The origins of the Zero Trust Framework are summarized in Figure 2.1.

For the longest time, businesses have adopted what is known as "Perimeter Security". A technical definition for it is as follows:

Perimeter security is the philosophy of setting up functional apparatus or techniques at the perimeter of the network to secure data and resources.

(Source: www.techopedia.com/definition/33764/
perimeter-security)

In other words, imagine one large circle encompassing a business, which is the main line of defense. That can be thought of as Perimeter Security. It is from within the confines of this circle that a business will deploy all of the firewalls, network intrusion devices, routers, etc., as well as other types of security technologies to fortify their defenses.

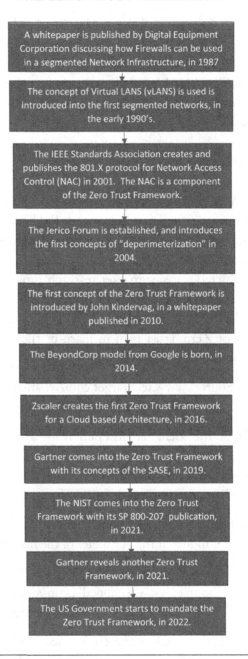

Figure 2.1   The Evolution of the Zero Trust Framework.

It is also at this point that the authentication mechanisms will be deployed, especially from the standpoint of Physical Access Entry. This is illustrated in Figure 2.2.

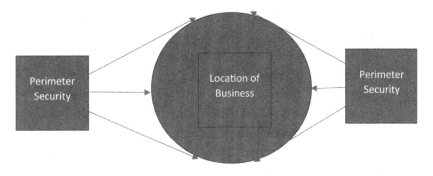

Figure 2.2 The Perimeter Defense Model.

With this kind of approach to security, there was always an implicit level of trust that was recognized. For example, if you were an employee gaining access to shared resources, it was always assumed that you went through all of the authentication processes that were in place. Even if you were a third-party vendor, the vetting process was very easy and simple to get through, because there was an implicit layer of trust that no intentional harm would ever be done to the datasets or the business processes that were being outsourced. In other words, the main concern was protecting the organization from threats that were coming from the external environment.

Nobody was really ever concerned about the internal environment of the business, because, after all, once again, if you were an employee, nobody really paid too much attention to your specific rights, permissions, and privileges. It was always assumed you were given the right amount to do your daily job tasks. Because of this, the thoughts of an Insider Attack from precipitating were pretty much null.

However, there is one major problem with the Perimeter Security approach. This model assumes only a layer of security. Thus, if the Cyberattacker were to penetrate through it, you then have pretty much given away the keys to the crown jewels of your company, because there are no other layers of security located from within the confines of the business.

There are other reasons for the eventual erosion of the Perimeter Security model, which are as follows:

1. *The Remote Workforce*:
   Many people thought that a 100% Remote Workforce would transpire later this decade. But, instead, the COVID-19

pandemic made this a reality within just a three-month timespan. With the influx of workers now working from home, there were many security issues that transpire. One of the largest ones was the intermingling of both the corporate network with the home-based networks. Gone were the days when an employee could simply log in to their workstation with their username and password. Now, with two different types Network Infrastructures touching base with another, remote employees now absolutely had to be confirmed with more than just one layer of authentication. As a result, many IT Security teams were left scrambling to implement a system where at least two or more layers of authentication would be required. This proved to be a major catalyst for the companies to start at least thinking about deploying the Zero Trust Framework in a serious manner.

2. *The Breakdown of the Virtual Private Network (VPN)*:
The VPN before the COVID-19 pandemic hit always provided a secure way for employees to remotely login into the servers where the shared resources were held. But, during these times, only about 25%–30% of employees were actually working remotely. But with the rapid influx to a near 99% Remote Workforce, the VPN started to show its breaking points. As a result, the Cyberattacker was able to exploit new weaknesses in a legacy system. Once again, using two or more layers of authentication and the concept of "Never Trust, Always Verify" took even further hold.

3. *The Race to the Cloud*:
Along with the issue of the intermingling of corporate and home-based networks, many remote employees were given company-issued devices that were not properly fitted with adequate security protocols installed onto them. Because of this, and other reasons, many businesses started to migrate their On-Premises Infrastructures into the major Cloud-based platforms, such as that of AWS and Microsoft Azure. Since this was an unknown territory for many organizations, especially for SMBs, many of them chose to utilize the Private Cloud deployment because of the security that was afforded. But, as familiarity with the Cloud started to settle

in, many of them subsequently started to move out to the Hybrid Cloud model. This is essentially a combination of the Private Cloud and Public Cloud. But, since lines access and separation were not too clear, many login credentials became at risk here, as the IT Security teams struggled to keep track of which end user (or employee) accounts needed to be created, and those which had to be deleted and/or deprovisioned. Even to this day, this is a big problem, as data leakage issues have emerged, especially with the AWS S3 buckets. This is an area now in which the IT Security teams are starting to realize which needs much more attention, especially through the use of automation. The use of Privileged Access Management (PAM) in a Zero Trust Framework is a solution, and, as mentioned earlier, it will be explored in more detail later in this chapter.

4. *Artificial Intelligence (AI) and Machine Learning (ML)*:
   The last couple of years has seen a huge rise in both of these technologies, especially when it comes to automation. This concept does not apply to manufacturing scenarios (this is where Robotic Process Automation comes into play), but it can also apply to virtual processes, such as when it comes to optimizing and parsing through large datasets (which is also known as "Big Data"). For example, if there is one Virtual Machine (VM) which has SQL Server running and another VM that is running an Oracle Enterprise database and they both are conducting automated tasks, there cannot be any kind of accidental data interchange between the two servers. Thus, only a Zero Trust Framework can help prevent this from happening, as these VMs are segregated from one another by their own boundaries.

The Demise of Perimeter Security

In the end, the ultimate goal of Perimeter Security was to keep all assets, whether they were digital, physical, or intellectual within the confines of the business, and the Perimeter Defense would contain them there and provide protection under just one layer of security. But, given the reasons in the last subsection, as well as other factors

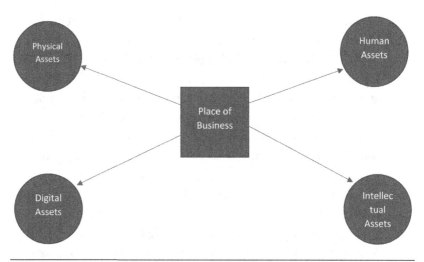

Figure 2.3 Distributed Assets.

(such as the rise of Insider Attacks and the overwhelming amount of threat variants from the external environment constantly pounding it), the demise of Perimeter Security finally happened.

Now, with offices and employees around the world and working in a virtual-based environment, the Perimeter Security Model will no longer suffice. This scattering of assets and resources for a company can be seen in Figure 2.3.

As a result, since everything is scattered all over the world, any kind of trust cannot be afforded anymore, thus fueling the demand for the Zero Trust Framework even more.

The Emergence of the Zero Trust Framework

So far in this chapter, we have provided a history of the evolution of the Zero Trust Framework and reviewed the factors that led to the eventual demise (or almost-near collapse) of the Perimeter Security Model. Thus going forward, we now assume that the Zero Trust Framework will be the methodology of choice for not only keeping the IT and Network Infrastructure secure for an organization but is also one of the most optimal ways in the authentication and authorization for end users (or employees) to gain access to shared resources and other types of confidential assets.

Before we resume with the initial Zero Trust Framework model we introduced at the end of Chapter 4, it is important some of the key properties of what truly makes up this framework. Some of these are as follows.

1. *It depends on risk*:
   Theoretically speaking, you want to protect everything that is at risk in your business. But, in a real-world sense, we know that this is totally infeasible. You can only give the highest levels of protection to those assets that are the most vulnerable to a security breach. Now, the question arises as to how to decide what is weak. One of the best ways to figure this out is for you and your IT Security team to take an inventory of all of the assets that your company has (both digital and physical) and break them down into the different categories that they belong to. Once this has been completed, you can then rank them on a scale, perhaps where 1 = Least Vulnerable and 10 = Most Vulnerable. Anything in the intermediate range would get a medium ranking. Now, you take all of those assets and from there determine the appropriate controls that they need. The bottom line here is that the depth of your Zero Trust Framework will be dependent upon how many vulnerable assets you have and how much they are worth that they have for the organization. Meaning if you have a lot of them, you will need to break out your IT and Network Infrastructure into more, smaller units. But if you are a smaller business, you may not have as many assets on hand, thus the need for segmentation will not be as high, and you will have a lesser amount of units that to be divided.

2. *Repeated use of MFA*:
   A constant theme throughout this book, especially in Chapters 3 and 4, has been the repeated use of MFA. For each and everything you need to access to, you must keep getting reauthenticated and reauthorized. This is also a core element of the Zero Trust Framework. While once again in theory this is probably the best way to fortify your lines of defense, following this procedure in the real world could prove to be very ineffective. For example, in the Public Key Infrastructure

(PKI) methodology that we have proposed, there will be an enormous drain on both resources and processing power. Therefore, one of the goals is to introduce Privileged Access Management (also known as "PAM"), which will allow the end user (or employee) to have to through the entire authentication and authorization only once. This will also be reviewed in greater detail later in this chapter.

3. *Endpoints are further protected*:

   One of the major pitfalls of the Perimeter Security Model is that Endpoint Security has often been a forgotten-about topic. Essentially, the endpoints are the points of origination and termination for the network lines of communication. Since they have been ignored for such a long period of time, this has been a favorite point of entry for the Cyberattacker to penetrate into IT and Network Infrastructure. As a result, they have been able to stay in for long periods of time and move laterally in a covert fashion. Because of this, they have also been to exfiltrate data a bit at a time, very often going unnoticed, until it was too late. But one of the strategic advantages of the Zero Trust Framework is that this is no longer an issue. In other words, Endpoint Security is a very crucial component that cannot be forgotten about.

4. *Isolation*:

   With the Perimeter Defense model, not only was it much easier for a Cyberattacker to get in, but it was also easier for them to get out of the system if they had been detected. However, this is not the case with the Zero Trust Framework. Because the IT and Network Infrastructure is broken up into different segments, it makes that much more difficult for the Cyberattacker to get through the crown jewels of the organization. But by the time he or she has broken through any lines of defense, the IT Security team will have alerted and remediation action will have followed immediately. Thus, there are very good chances that the Cyberattacker will be isolated with no point of exit possible.

5. *Finer levels of control*:

   Under Perimeter Defense, for the most part, the concept of Least Privilege was followed. But most of the rights, permissions, and privileges were of a "macro" one, meaning that it was quite possible for an end user (or employee) to still access other applications when they had no reason to. In other words, people were put into various groups and profiles in an Active Directory structure with the rights, permissions, and privileges already preestablished in it. There were no finer controls established to prevent unintended access to other systems. This becomes especially crucial for those Privileged Accounts. Thus, another key mandate of the Zero Trust Framework is to establish a granular (or finer) set of controls that will eliminate this kind of cross-over to other applications.

6. *Comprehensive auditing*:

    Most companies set up their Perimeter Security to only audit certain parts of their IT Network Infrastructures. Most of them were set up to monitor the flow of network traffic in and out of the business and to detect any rouge data packets. It wasn't until recently that the interest in detecting malicious or unusual behavior picked up with the advent of both AI and ML tools. But, with the Zero Trust Framework, and especially for those deployed in a Cloud-based environment, there are now tools available that give the IT Security team the ability to audit everything in their respective infrastructures. This also includes the ever-important endpoints, and even the ability to track a wireless device on a real-time basis, and even obtain a log file from that. Also with Perimeter Defense, the IT Security team traditionally had to comb through all of the log files that were outputted on a manual basis. Compounding this fact was that security tools came from different vendors, and, as a result of that, different formats were created. But now, and with the growth of the Zero Trust Framework, a central console can be used (which is a Security Incident Event Manager, or "SIEM" for short) to see the outputs of all of the log files from one central location.

7. *The use of adaptive control*:

    The common way to detect any sort of malicious or rogue behavior under the Perimeter Security Model was to create a simple baseline and, from there, upon the thresholds set by the IT Security team, anything outside of what was deemed to be normal would require further attention. But this would often trigger what is known as "false positives". To alleviate this situation, there are other variables that have to be taken into account to determine true, rogue behavior. These are as follows:

- Time of the day
- Day of the week
- Geographic location
- IP Address
- Target Server
- Target Application

These kinds of specifications are more or less required by a Zero Trust Framework and are to be conducted on a real-time basis. The variables just examined earlier are also technically known as "Adaptive Controls".

8. *Contextual request*:

With implicit trust being used in a Perimeter Defense Model, any elevation of privileges, rights, and permissions was often granted without a second thought, especially for the privileged accounts. But since the Zero Trust Framework means absolutely no trust whatsoever, the granting of super-user permissions can take place only if only questions such as the entity who is requesting this, the target server, why this kind of access is needed, and for how long it will be required have all been answered.

9. *Lateral movement*:

Since there are many layers of security in the Zero Trust Framework, the lateral movement of a Cyberattacker is almost nil after even penetrating the first one or two layers. This is unlike the Perimeter Defense Model, where, after piercing through the first and only line of defense, the Cyberattacker will have complete reign in the IT and Network Infrastructure.

The Basic Zero Trust Framework Model

Now that we have reviewed some of the most properties of the Zero Trust Framework, it is now at this point we actually present the basic model of the Zero Trust Framework. Once again, keep that this is a

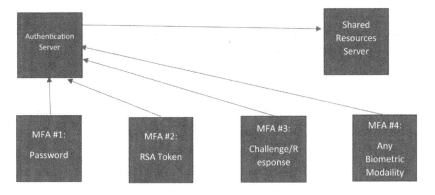

Figure 2.4 A Model of the Zero Trust Framework and Multifactor Authentication (MFA).

methodology and it is not meant to be a cookie-cutter approach to security. Businesses can modify it, by making additions to it as they see necessary (Figure 2.4).

This can be deemed to be the most fundamental model of the Zero Trust Framework. For example, first embraces MFA, in which at least three more mechanisms are used. In the previous scenario, there are four of them and there are three types of identification criteria that are met in this case, which are as follows:

1. *Something you are*:
   This is typically something that is permanent about you, such as your physiological or behavioral self. This is where Biometrics (reviewed in Chapter 3) will come into play (which is MFA #4).
2. *Something you know*:
   This is a piece of information and/or data that you know of. It can be a password, an answer to a challenge/response question, and so on. These are represented as MFA #1, and MFA #3, respectively.
3. *Something you have*:
   This is something in your position such as an RSA Token, smartcard, FOB, etc. This is represented as MFA #2.

Once the end user (or employee) has gone through all of these iterations, he or she will then be granted access to whatever shared resources they need to conduct their daily job tasks. But the caveat here is that each end user wants to gain access to something else or different, they have to go through this entire process once again. And, if this happens multiple times in a single day (which is highly probable), then it will not only be a cumbersome process, but it can be a drain of processing power on the part of the Authentication Server.

In our proposed model of the Zero Trust Framework, we theoretically do away with this repetitive cycle by making use of the concepts of Privileged Access Management (PAM). As mentioned, this will be reviewed in more detail later in this chapter.

Because of the almost-near eradication of the Perimeter Defense Model, this has left many businesses in what is called an "amorphous state". Meaning, there are no clear-cut boundaries as to where all of the digital assets now lie; they are now technically speaking in different physical locations, but, virtually, they look like they are all in one place if you are using a Cloud-based deployment. This now gives rise to a very important concept for the traditional Zero Trust Framework Model: Segmentation.

What Is Segmentation?

When one thinks of this concept, the image of a large unit being broken into smaller bits often comes to mind. This is true of the Zero Trust Framework. A technical definition of Segmentation is as follows:

> It is a network security technique that divides a network into smaller, distinct sub-networks that enable network teams to compartmentalize the sub-networks and deliver unique security controls and services to each sub-network.
>
> The process of network segmentation involves partitioning a physical network into different logical sub-networks. Once the network has been subdivided into smaller more manageable units, controls are applied to the individual, compartmentalized segments.
>
> (Source: www.vmware.com/topics/glossary/content/
> network-segmentation.html).

Although the entire processes and operation of a business can be broken into smaller units or segments, it is typically the IT and Network Infrastructure that is broken down, because it is deemed to be the most vital component (or "heart and soul") of any enterprise. So now imagine all of those digital assets (this can be everything from the databases to the Virtual Machines to the Virtual Desktops to all of the datasets, etc.) that are now in existence in any kind of Cloud deployment (again, they are the Private, Public, and Hybrid Clouds).

Per the permutations and requirements that have been set forth by the IT Security team and the CISO, all of them now will reside in smaller units or what will now be termed "Segments". Each of these segments will be surrounded by its own boundary, with all of the authentication mechanisms which support the MFA protocols. In more technical terms, these can also be referred to as "Subnets", as alluded to in the previous definition. These Segments can still be, on a theoretical level, broken down into smaller ones, which become known as "Microsegments".

It is important to note at this point that this model of the Zero Trust Framework (and even those going forward) requires that the authentication methods that are being used *be different from one another.* This means that, for each boundary that encompasses a certain Segment, all the MFA mechanisms used must be totally different from one another. For example, one could still be a password, one can be a smart card, and the other be a Biometric.

But the only caveat here is that there are a finite number of authentication mechanisms that can go around. But, even with this, there are still quite a number of possibilities in which you can set up your MFA strategies. For example, you could take the MFA from one layer and use three layers up or down in the segmented IT/Network Infrastructure. Also, the Zero Trust Framework mandates that the same authentication methods for supporting the MFA should not be used for long periods of time. They once again should follow a regular schedule of randomization by swapping them out to a preestablished plan.

Probably the most important keywords to remember with the Zero Trust Framework are that of Trajectory and Isolation. With the former, even though the Cyberattacker might be able to break through one or two, and perhaps even three layers of defense, the chances of he or she getting to the proverbial crown jewels become almost statistically nil. With the latter, once a Cyberattacker has broken through, the chances of him or her breaking out again are also almost nil again,

Figure 2.5   A 3 Dimensional Model of IT/Network Segmentation.

because they will be facing the issue of Isolation because of the other layers of defense that will be surrounding them.

Figure 2.5 gives a three-dimensional view of what segmentation looks like.

However, this basic model of the Zero Trust Framework does not include the following components of our proposed model:

1. The Public Key Infrastructure
2. Privileged Access Management
3. BioCryptography
4. Quantum Mechanics.

As mentioned previously, these four components will be examined in more detail toward the end of this chapter. But while we are still on this theme of the basic Zero Trust Framework model, the next sections of this chapter will cover the following topics:

- The advantages/disadvantages of the Zero Trust Framework
- Best practices in deploying a basic Zero Trust Framework Model at your business.

The Advantages of the Zero Trust Framework

Although the basic model of the Zero Trust Framework may sound very complex in nature because of all of the Segmenting that will be going on and all of the MFA authentication mechanisms that will be deployed, once it is established, it won't appear to be that way. But the key here is that whatever Zero Trust Framework Model you deploy, it will have to be deployed in phases. It simply cannot be implemented all at once, as grave mistakes are sure to happen.

Best Practices of the Zero Trust Framework

In fact, there will be a section later in this chapter that will outline some of the best practices that you can take to deploy the basic model of the Zero Trust Framework. But, despite how complex it may look from the outset, there are a number of key advantages that will far outweigh even the ones that are found with the Perimeter Defense Model. Here are some of the benefits of the Zero Trust Framework:

1. *Both kinds of threats are mitigated*:
   By this, we mean the threats from both the external and internal environments. While the Perimeter Defense Model can do a sufficient job with the former for a period of time, it does not offer a means by which threats from the internal environment can tracked. By this, we mean Insider Attacks. This kind of threat vector can stem from any kind of source, but the common denominator here is that it usually takes an employee from the inside to launch this kind of attack. After all, they know best the internal workings of a company (this depends on their specific job role), and they will, of course, have some idea as to where the damage can be initiated. For example, this can be an employee who feels that they are about to lose their job, or, through a Social Engineering tactic, there could be somebody from the outside world conning an employee to launch such a threat vector. Under traditional security practices, it is very difficult to detect the beginning of an Insider Attack. At best, the log files will alert the IT Security team for unusual behavior, but this is really not enough to tell with accuracy if anything is about to happen. But with the Zero Trust Framework, the key here is to protect not only from threat vectors that are posed by the external environments *but from those that are internal as well.*

Given all the internal boundaries and the many authentication mechanisms, it will be a lot easier now to detect the precipitation of an Insider Attack. In other words, with the Zero Trust Framework, the business is protected from different kinds of environments, which is a huge advantage to have.

2. *Can see all of the actions*:

Before the COVID-19 pandemic hit, a lot of the IT Security teams did not pay too much attention to the kinds of types of devices that the employees were using, although they should have been. But once it happened, the fears then quickly arose about who was accessing what through which device, driven primarily because of the intermeshing of both the business and home networks. Another trigger point for this Bring Your Own Device (BYOD) was remote employees were very often using their own personal devices to conduct their daily job tasks rather than making use of company-issued equipment. With the Zero Trust Framework, a much closer eye can be kept on the devices that are being used to access the shared resources. This is so because each device must now be registered with the IT Security team, and, since MFA will be used, it will be much more difficult for employees to access anything through their personal devices. Also, since all network-based activities can be seen through a central console, the IT Security team will now be able to track down lost or stolen devices and from that point issue a "Remote Wipe" command to permanently delete any confidential information or data that may have been stored on it. Remember that in the end.

3. *Reduction in data loss*:

This has always been an issue, even before the COVID-19 pandemic hit. But once it was completely unleashed, the issue of data leakage, whether intentional or not, became a much graver concern. For example, most of the home networks that were being used to access the business network were using only a password as the primary means of defense. This constituted a weak defense, at best. As a result, the Cyberattacker could very easily have broken through this line of access and moved laterally into the business network. From here, depending upon where they were at, they could then stay in long enough to see where the datasets reside and which ones were the most valuable to exfiltrate. Of course, they are not going to do all of this at once; they are going to take out these datasets a bit at a time, to go unnoticed. But, if the Zero Trust Framework had been implemented during this time frame, the fear of data loss would have been greatly diminished, because of all of the layers of defenses that the Cyberattacker would have to literally go through. Plus, each defense layer will also have its own set of controls, thus making data loss/exfiltration an almost impossible task to accomplish.

4. *Security is better in the Cloud*:

As it has been mentioned throughout this book, many organizations have been moving to the Cloud and migrating their On-Premises Infrastructures totally into it. Not only does it afford monthly pricing, but one of the key strategies is that it is highly scalable. For example, if you do have a Zero Trust Framework that is in the Cloud, it is quite easy to break out new assets into their own distinctive segments, as well as deploy the appropriate MFA protocols and authentication mechanisms into place. If, for some reason any assets have to be deleted or deprovisioned, the Zero Trust Framework will adjust accordingly, on an automatic basis without any human intervention involved. Also, the major Cloud providers, especially that of Microsoft Azure, already have a suite of MFA tools that can be installed and deployed with just a few clicks of the mouse. However, it should be noted that the debate between having a Zero Trust Framework in the Cloud versus it being On-Premises will always be a continuing one. But making changes to it with the latter will obviously take longer, which is something no organization can afford. Thus, the choice is quite clear in this regard.

5. *A newer type of Workforce Model*:

The workforce when the COVID-19 pandemic hit was almost all remote based. This meant that people could work from anywhere, in their homes, or even in any other public location, as long as there was a secure Internet connection. But, as the pandemic started to ease down, many businesses started to reopen their doors. However, a majority of the remote employees preferred to work from the physical location of their office only a few days a week. Thus, this gave birth to a newer type of workforce model, called the "Hybrid Model", where the remote worker would spend one or two days in the office and the rest of the time would be spent working from home. Because of this, many of these businesses then transferred their Cloud deployment to a Hybrid one as well. With this kind of approach, if a Perimeter Defense Model were to be used, it would be much more difficult to keep track of all of where all the devices were being used and which end user (or employee) was accessing which shared resources. But, by using the Cloud, the Zero Trust Framework can easily keep track of these geographically separated devices and ensure that MFA is still being used on them. But the only issue here is keeping track of all of the accounts and profiles in the Azure Activity Directory. This is where the role of Privileged Access Management (PAM) will come into play.

6. *Supports compliance across the board*:
   The world today is filled with various data privacy laws. Some of the most well-known ones are those of the GDPR, the CCPA, and HIPAA. Depending upon their revenue and employee size, companies will have to come under the tight scrutiny of regulators from each of these laws. If the right controls are not in place or there are any data leakage issues, the company will be in the crosshairs for an audit and possible steep financial penalties. But, with the Zero Trust Framework, since there are so many controls and authentication mechanisms put into place (especially if you are using a Cloud-based deployment), there is a much greater chance that you will more or less be in compliance with these various data privacy laws and experience a much lower risk of data exfiltration issues.

The Disadvantages of the Zero Trust Framework

Despite the strategic advantages that the Zero Trust Framework brings to an organization, it has its set of disadvantages as well. Some of these include the following:

1. *It is viewed as extreme*:

   To an end user (or an employee), the Zero Trust Framework is often perceived as going way too far to the other extreme in security. But, unfortunately, despite all of the best efforts to provide employees with security awareness training and trying to keep up with the Cyber Threat landscape, there is really no other choice. There is a lot at stake here for the CISO, as well as other members of the C-Suite and even the Board of Directors, which are, namely, the protection of the digital assets and the confidential datasets of both the employees and the customers. The situation of Zero Trust has been for a lack of a better term, forced upon us, given the dynamics that we are facing today. We simply cannot take anything for granted anymore, because the Cyberattacker has also become a lot stealthier and covert in the way they launch their threat vectors. Some of the people who will feel the worst brunt of the Zero Trust Framework will be those who have been around the longest in a company. Given their long tenure, there is obviously a lot of trust that has been placed in them. But to have that taken all that taken away at once and then not trust them at all (from the standpoint of authentication and authorization) can be traumatic. Therefore, one of the key aspects when deploying a Zero Trust Framework is to keep a direct line of communications open with the end users (or employees) and all levels of management and vice versa. It is very important to get their buy-in even to the slightest degree possible and explain the benefits of what it is all about. If this is not done properly, resentment toward the Zero Trust Framework will get even worse and your end users (or employees) may try to circumvent the system altogether, thus defeating its very purpose. One way to alleviate this situation is to deploy your Zero Trust Framework in phases, as was pointed out earlier in this chapter. By taking this kind of approach, you will be giving your end users (or employees) a time period to digest the new changes that will be happening to them. Although it may take a lot longer to completely build out your Zero Trust Framework to its entirety, the slower the pace the better, at least from the standpoint of end user (or employee) adoption.

2. *The use of Microsegmentation*:
   As it was explained in great detail, the use of the Zero Trust Framework relies heavily upon the concept of Segmentation. Once again, this is where the entire IT and Network Infrastructure is divided up into separate segments, with each of them being surrounded by its own boundary and MFA authentication tools. But, if the organization is a very large one, and if the Zero Trust Framework has proven to be successful, the CISO and the IT Security team could consider making use of what is known as "Microsegmentation". This is where the given Segment is broken down into an even smaller one. A benefit of this of course is an extra added layer of security. But if it is deployed for no other reason, it can cause more complications to an already-existing Zero Trust Framework. Therefore, any other major tweaks or adjustments like this should be done only if there is some success that has been proven with it initially. In other words, don't add any more to your Zero Trust Framework until it has given you a positive ROI for the time and money you have spent on it initially.

3. *A mix of environments*:
   Although many organizations have made their full shift to the Cloud, there are some still out there that are hesitant to do this, so they have resorted to what is known as a "Mixed Model". This is where they may use part of the Cloud for some of their IT and Network Infrastructure, and the rest still remains On-Prem. While this approach may work for some time, it is certainly not a suitable one for the Zero Trust Framework. In other words, it can't be deployed in half in one environment and half in another kind. It has to

be implemented fully and in only one type of environment. One of the reasons for this is that it will be a lot harder to keep track of all of the MFA mechanisms that are in place, as well as the accesses that are being made to the shared resources. Therefore, before even starting to deploy a Zero Trust Framework, you as the CISO, and your IT Security team need to assess the best kind of environment a Zero Trust Framework will work for you. Then you need to plan accordingly. But, if there are any lingering thoughts about making a full migration to the Cloud, you should do that first and then consider the creation of a Zero Trust Framework. But it is also important to keep in mind that a Zero Trust Framework may not even be a viable solution for some businesses, especially those that are classified as a "Small Business" (around 15 employees or less). In these cases, perhaps just using a Two Factor Authentication (2FA) could work as well.

4. *Some flexibility is required*:
   Although the Zero Trust Framework is inherently designed to be a tight-knit kind of environment, there may be some degree of flexibility that is needed in the initial outlay of it, as your end users (or employees) are starting to get used to a brand-new way of accessing resources that they need. But you and your IT Security team should not let your guard down, as this could be a pivotal moment for the Cyberattacker to penetrate into walls of defense. But, even after this, depending upon the job roles that your remote employees have, there may be a need for some flexibility. This will be especially true for those that are deemed to be the "Road Warriors" and need access to applications and/or resources they need immediately which they never had before.

5. *The IoT*:
   This is an acronym that stands for the "Internet of Things". Essentially, this is where all of the objects that we interact with in both the physical and digital worlds are all interconnected together. While the IoT has a certain number of key advantages for personal applications (such as the "Smarthome" and the "Smart Car"), it can pose a serious

threat to business applications and processes and even to the Zero Trust Framework. The primary reason for this is that many of the interconnections in the world of the IoT are often insecure, as they remain unencrypted. In other words, any communications that take place between devices and any authentication/authorization credentials (such as your user-name/password and PIN number) are sent as a "Cleartext", which is decipherable to anybody. If this were to be intercepted by a malicious third party, just about anything disastrous could happen. Also, if any of these IoT devices were connected to a Zero Trust Framework without any prior authorization from the IT Security team, this could yet be another avenue for the Cyberattacker to get in, at least through the first layer of defense.

Now that we have reviewed some of the key advantages and disadvantages of the Zero Trust Framework, we now turn our attention over to a set of best practices that should be at least taken into consideration when deploying its basic model.

Some of the Best Practices

Although the Zero Trust Framework model we have been reviewing thus far in this chapter has been the basic one, there are still a number of key points to keep in mind when you deploy it. Also, remember that this methodology is not designed to be a "one size fits all". Meaning what will work for one environment will not work for yours. As mentioned, a lot will depend upon the Risk Assessment that you and your IT Security team have compiled at a previous point in time and the appropriate set of controls you have decided upon as a result.

Here are some of these key tips:

1. *Form a Zero Trust Team*:
   Before you even start to draft a plan for deploying the Zero Trust Framework at your organization, you first need to create a team with the key stakeholders in mind. Obviously, this will consist of you, the CISO, and a representative member of the IT Security team. Keep in mind that this

is a methodology which will have an impact on everybody in the business. Therefore, it would be best to also include a representative from the other departments as well. Perhaps even consider including a member of the C-Suite and the IT Department as well. The purpose of this team is to address all of the concerns and needs of the organization and how you plan to start the buy-in process from the other employees. Although in theory the Zero Trust Framework in theory can be used by any business, in practicality, it may not be the most suitable approach for a business. Therefore, this is something that should be discussed as well before moving forward. Also, the impacts of a Zero Trust Framework on the technological components and the digital assets that your organization has need to be taken into very serious consideration as well. But this is a more urgent matter if you still have an On-Premises Infrastructure. If you have a Cloud-based deployment, then this topic may not be as important to discuss, as templates and strategies should be available to you from your Cloud Provider to guide you with this process.

2. *Assess the environments that you are in*:
   By this, if you are 100% in the Cloud, you and your IT Security team need to take a very accurate stock of where digital assets are at in terms of the deployments that you are using. For example, is all of your IT and Network Infrastructure located in just the Private, Hybrid, or Public Cloud, or is it segregated among all three or just two of them? Or if you are still using an On-Premises Infrastructure, in which areas do you have your servers, workstations, and wireless devices? From here, it is important to create a high-level map as to where everything is located. This will then form the foundation as to how you will create the various Segments in your IT and Network Infrastructure. Another key advantage of using the Cloud is that you will have tools at your disposal to map this out fairly quickly.

3. *Decide the authentication tools*:
   If after completing the first two steps the decision is a "yes" to go with the creation of a Zero Trust Framework, then an

important next step is to decide upon the kinds and types of authentication mechanisms that you and your IT Security team think will work best for the security requirements of your company. Some of the favored ones are the use of passwords, challenge/response questions, smart cards, FOBs, RSA tokens, Biometrics, and so on. In fact, with some of these tools, there will be other complimentary tools that you can use as well. For example, there are other technologies that are similar to the RSA token and you can use those in conjunction with RSA one as well. Although we have detailed the Biometric modalities of choice for a Zero Trust Framework in Chapter 3, there are still others that you can choose from, but keep in mind that they are not all commercially available yet. Another important tool that you can give serious consideration to and which is widely available is known as the "SASE". This is an acronym that stands for "Secure Access Service Edge". This is a SaaS-based device that creates and deploys a VM near the devices that are requesting access to the shared resources and processing of data. The idea is that, by having it closer to the end user (or employee), the transmission and transaction times will be quicker. A theoretical illustration of the SASE is illustrated in Figure 2.6.

4. *Develop your Zero Trust Framework Plan:*
   Once you have decided on the authentication mechanisms as reviewed, the next step is to actually map how your Zero Trust Framework will look, going into the granular detail as much as possible. Think of this as the security

Figure 2.6   The SASE Concept.

blueprint for your company. In this set of documents, you should establish every Segment in your IT and Network Infrastructure, as well as the authentication tools that will be used. There are two key things to keep in mind here:

- This set of documents is still theoretical in nature. So far they have not been tested in a real-world environment. Therefore, you and your IT Security team need to literally test each and every Segment in a sandbox-like environment to make sure that it is working up to expectations and that there are no glitches which are involved. If there are any, then it must be remediated immediately. Once one Segment has been deemed optimal, it can be released into the production environment where your end users (or employees) will start the MFA approach to gain access to the shared resources that they are seeking.

- By taking the previous approach, you will actually be developing the plan as to how will phase in your Zero Trust Framework. True, you and your IT Security team can test all of the Segments in the sandbox all at once and deploy them into production that same way, but errors are prone to happen, which could have a detrimental cascading effect on the other layers of security. Therefore, and as also stated previously in this chapter, the Zero Trust Framework must be implemented in steps, or in phases, to minimize any kind of downtime to your business. So the bottom line here is to test each component separately and then deploy it.

5. *The complete deployment*:

At some point in time, after all of the diagramming, documentation, and testing, your Zero Trust Framework should be up and running in its full entirety. But keep in mind that it does not end there. Rather, you and your IT Security team, as well as the other key stakeholders (as identified in the first step), need to keep a close eye on how things are working. If there are any issues (there will most likely be some in the first few months of actual deployment), they need to be investigated and rectified immediately before they are transmitted to the other segments of the Zero Trust Framework, if at all. Each Segment will be independent of this, so this risk should be minimal in terms of actual occurrence. But, apart from this, your team should also be kept apprised of other new kinds of tools which emerge in the marketplace that could potentially be used in a Zero Trust Framework. Keep in mind that you want your model to be as updated as possible in terms of newer technologies, as well as having a regular software patch/update schedule for your authentication mechanisms. In fact, if it is feasible for your organization, you may even want to consider having a dedicated Zero Trust Framework team whose primary purpose is to keep tabs on what is going on and make recommendations for improvement.

6. *Always seek approval*:
   As your Zero Trust Framework Model continues to evolve throughout your business, keep in mind that changes and refinements will always be made do it to keep up with the latest threat vectors that are appearing on the Cyber landscape. But one cannot simply change something when they want to. Rather there has to be a solid system of checks and balances in place. This is where the Change Configuration Committee comes into place. Every request for a change or an upgrade must be brought up and approved at this level. Any action taken must also be documented, not only for the sake of compliance but to also abide by the tenets of the various data privacy laws (such as the GDPR, CCPA, and HIPAA).

Keep in mind that there are also key metrics that you can use to gauge the true effectiveness of your Zero Trust Framework Model. Some of these include the following:

1. *Mean time to detect (MTTD)*:
   This is a crucial element because the faster an organization identifies an attack, the greater the odds it can contain it with minimal damage.

2. *Mean time to respond (MTTR)*:
   The ability to neutralize a threat and get systems back online is critical because as events drag out, risks and costs increase.
3. *Mean time to contain (MTTC)*:
   This metric refers to the average time required to shut down all attack vectors across all endpoints and minimize the probability of any further damage.

(Source: www.mimecast.com/blog/top-10-cybersecurity-metrics-and-kpis/)

The Flaws with the Traditional Zero Trust Framework Model

Up to this point in this chapter, we have reviewed the history of the basic Zero Trust Framework model, as well as the Perimeter Defense Model. As was noted earlier, many businesses are now shying away from this, as it is not a robust tool to be using anymore. Various reasons were also pointed out as to how the basic Zero Trust Framework can overcome the shortcomings of the Perimeter Defense model. The various of the former were examined, as well as its strengths and advantages.

Finally, a set of best practices were also reviewed in detail. But, believe it or not, despite the basic Zero Trusts Framework "overpowering" the Perimeter Defense model, it still has its own set of shortcomings as well. Thus, at the end of Chapter 4, we proposed our own version of the Zero Trust Framework, which we believe can overcome the weaknesses of the basic one. To summarize, here are weaknesses of it:

1. The use of MFA authentication mechanisms which can still be the target of the Cyberattacker.
2. Having the end user (or employee) keep verifying, and going through all of the authentication and authorization processes over and over again, each and every time they need access to shared resources.
3. No integrity checks are being conducted as authentication information, and data are being transmitted to the authorization server, which grants the end user (or employee) access to the shared resources.

4. Still heavy dependence on using the password as one of the prime mechanisms for the MFA methodology.

Keep in mind that the Zero Trust Framework is designed to work in the internal environment of an organization. It is not all designed to work in the external environment.

3

THE COMPONENTS OF
PRIVILEGED ACCESS
MANAGEMENT

What Exactly Is PAM?

The technical definition of PAM is as follows:

> Privileged access management (PAM) is the combination of tools and technology used to secure, control and monitor access to an organization's critical information and resources. Subcategories of PAM include shared access password management, privileged session management, vendor privileged access management (VPAM) and application access management.

> (Source: www.techtarget.com/searchsecurity/definition/ privileged-access-management-PAM)

So as you can see from the definition, PAM is all about securing the login credentials of individuals. But it is not just used for anybody. Rather, the concepts of PAM are specifically designed to help protect those accounts that are deemed to have access to the crown jewels of a business. This could include a wide range of titles, including the members of the Board of Directors and the C-Suite, all those titles such as Network Administrator, Database Administrator, and members of the IT Security team.

The reason why these PAM-based accounts get so much attention is that these are the kinds of credentials that the Cyberattacker goes after the most. After all, if they can hijack these kinds of credentials, they will be able to get to the most prized possessions very easily and quickly, without having to further penetrate the IT and Network Infrastructure for an extended period of time.

Other examples of PAM-based accounts include the following:

- Security procedures, which include Incident Response, Disaster Recovery, and Business Continuity Plans.
- Local administrative accounts.
- Access to the Azure Active Directory (AAD).
- Any applications or services.
- Administrative accounts dealing with domains and web-based applications.

PAM is also very important because it helps ensure that organizations come into compliance with various data privacy laws such as those of the CCPA, GDPR, and HIPAA. All of the PAM accounts, for the most part, are grouped into what are known as "System Administrator" accounts. The idea here is to separate them from the other login credentials of the employees.

The Features of a PAM Service

Some of the major components of PAM include the following:

1. *Multifactor Authentication (MFA) for administrators*:
   As it was reviewed in the previous chapters of this book, this is where at least three or more layers of authentication are used to confirm the identity of the individual. It is imperative that different authentication mechanisms be used.
2. *An access manager that stores permissions and privileged user information*:
   These are the secrets that are stored in a safe area in the PAM environment. The goal here is to get rid of passwords as much as possible.
3. *A password vault that stores secured, privileged passwords*:
   If passwords have to be used (thus theoretically defeating the purpose of a PAM system), then the vault is where they must be stored. This is deemed to be the safest and most secure area in the PAM system.
4. *Session tracking once privileged access is granted*:
   Once the PAM account has been activated, it must be watched closely so that there is no misuse of it, whether by the account itself or even by a Cyberattacker.

5. *Dynamic authorization abilities*:

   Once a PAM account has been assigned, it must only last when it is absolutely necessary and needed. In this regard, it is almost an impossible task for an IT Security team to do this all the time, so AI and ML tools will be needed for automation.

6. *Automated provisioning and deprovisioning to reduce insider threats*:

   Once the PAM account is not needed, it can be either deprovisioned or deleted. This must happen immediately when the account is no longer needed. It is always best to delete the PAM account altogether, from the standpoint of Cybersecurity. Once again, automation is needed here, with the help of AI and ML.

7. *A tools that help organizations meet compliance*:

   One of the main audit areas of regulators for data privacy laws is to make sure that all of the needed and required controls are in place to protect all login credentials. This is one of the other components of PAM that is strongly needed in today's world.

The Challenges of an On-Site PAM Solution

Before the huge explosion into the Cloud took place over the last couple of years, many businesses had their PAM-based solutions on site. They were faced with many issues, which included the following:

1. *Manage account credentials*:

   Unlike the Cloud-based PAM solutions, On-Prem solutions require that everything has to be stored in a central location. This of course caused huge problems, especially if the Cyberattacker was able to break through. But with a Cloud-based PAM, there can be multiple storage locations which can be dispersed in different geographic locations around the world.

2. *Track privileged activity*:

   Any usage of the PAM account had to be done on a manual basis. Of course, as the business environment has become more complex, this is no longer a feasible alternative, thus making the Cloud-based PAM a very strong alternative.

3. *Monitor and analyze threats:*

   With On-Prem PAM solutions, there really is no tool that can be plugged into it to constantly watch over any malicious activity taking place on the PAM account. But with the Cloud-based PAM solutions, an SIEM can be plugged into it very quickly and alert the IT Security team of any abnormal behavior. Best yet, with the help of AI and ML, false positives can be easily filtered out.

4. *Control privileged user access:*

   With the On-Prem PAM solutions, all accounts have to be created and deprovisioned quickly, and this was done on a manual basis (and still continues to be the case). As stated earlier, this takes too much time away from the IT Security team, and because of that, many PAM accounts go unmonitored. This of course without a doubt is a huge security risk. But with a Cloud-based PAM solution, and by using AI and ML, this is all mitigated and done on an automated basis. The end result here is that no PAM account will be forgotten about. Everything can be created, deprovisioned, and/or adjusted within the preestablished timeframes and permutations.

5. *Balance security with ease of use:*

   There is no doubt that On-Prem-based solutions are totally cumbersome and take a lot of trial and error to not only install but make sure that they fit into your security requirements. But, in stark contrast, Cloud-based PAM solutions are just the opposite. The primary reason for this is that many of the PAM vendors of today are making their products come with a strong sense of ease of use for the IT Security team.

Vendor-Based PAM

In today's digital world, businesses in Corporate America are now relying more than ever before on third-party vendors, to fulfill mission-critical business operations. This dependency has been greater now than it has ever been. But with the way the threat environment is going, a CISO simply cannot have implicit trust in a vendor, blindly follow them, and outsource all of the confidential information and data to them. There has to be a strict vetting process in place, and in this regard, the Zero Trust Framework, in a different way, also applies here as well.

In other words, you simply cannot trust, you have to keep verifying, even when it comes to hiring a third-party vendor. To this extent, the major PAM vendors have now included various safeguards in their solutions to help protect any accidental or intentional data leakages from a third-party vendor. These solutions are especially known as "VPAM", which is an acronym for "Vendor Privileged Access Management". Here are the major components that are included:

1. *Identification and authentication*:
   Third-party vendor access is difficult to manage because of the lack of oversight by the IT Security team. As a result, implementing and deploying MFA and other sorts of vendor identity management techniques become of paramount importance. One of the primary benefits of VPAM tools is that they can provide customized authentication options which can easily offboard and onboard users. This component prevents third-party vendors that exit the company from taking their access with them.

2. *Access Control*:
   A VPAM-based solution gives the CISO and the IT Security team the ability to implement permissions and create an efficient working system to meet a strict set of requirements for a selected third-party vendor. For example, Access Control can be as granular as using the concept of Least Privilege or as macro as allowing access to an entire network application. The IT Security team can also schedule access by supervised or unsupervised Access Control at times convenient for monitoring, adding to the efficiency and security of an enterprise network.

3. *Recording and auditing*:
   As mentioned earlier in this chapter, VPAM tools make use of both AI and ML as an automated process to monitor user activity during every session and can documented. This is typically done in a log file and records the who, what, where, when, and why of any remote support session. An audit benefit of this is that a VPAM platform also means that businesses can ensure vendor accountability and compliance with industry regulations.

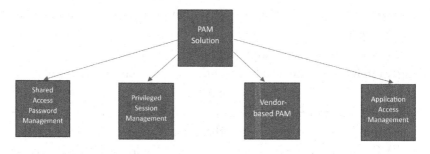

Figure 3.1   A Virtual Privileged Access Management (PAM) Model.

These components can be seen in Figure 3.1.

With many more businesses now adopting the usage of PAM-based Cloud solutions, there is now a lot of confusion as to the differences between what PAM and Identity Access Management (also known as "IAM") are all about. The technical definition of Identity Access Management is as follows:

> Identity and access management (IAM) is a cybersecurity discipline focused on managing user identities and access permissions on a computer network. While IAM policies, processes, and technologies can differ between companies, the goal of any IAM initiative is to ensure that the right users and devices can access the right resources for the right reasons at the right time.

(Source: www.ibm.com/topics/identity-access-management)

So as you can see from the definition, Identity and Access Management provides security policies on a macro level, such as when it comes to dealing with an entire IT and Network Infrastructure. But PAM deals strictly with Privileged Accounts, no matter where the repositories and vaults are stored. Simply put, while some overlap exists, PAM is strictly focused on accounts with privileged or administrative access On the contrary, Identity Access Management encompasses any users that require access to a system. For example, it provides organizations with a way to authenticate and authorize general access to employees, partners, and customers.

To ensure the highest level of security, companies should seriously consider deploying and implementing both Privileged Access Management and Identity Access Management. For example, the former covers larger attack surfaces within the organization's network, while PAM systems cover smaller, higher-valued attack surfaces.

The Different Types of PAM Accounts

Non-Privileged Accounts

Up to this point, we have reviewed in some detail what PAM is about and its main functionalities. The heart of this is the Privileged Accounts. Therefore, in this section, we do a deeper dive into what actually the kinds and types of PAM accounts which exist.

First, it is very important to start with what a Non-Privileged Account is all about. Essentially, these are general-purpose accounts given to all of the employees of a company that do not require privileged access. In this regard, the concept of Least Privilege should be strictly observed, in which the employees are given just what they need to conduct their daily job functions, no more and no less. The following are types of Non-Privileged Accounts:

1. *The Standard User Accounts*:
   These kinds and types of accounts meet the needs of typical employees: email, web browsing, and word processing, plus role-based access to SaaS tools for communication and project management.
2. *Guest User Accounts*:
   These accounts have limited privileges, including basic application access and internet browsing. This is what is typically used for contractors, third-party suppliers, and other external users and entities.

Privileged Accounts for End Users

The total number of Privileged Accounts that you will need for your business is dependent upon a number of key factors, which include the following:

- Your security requirements.
- The kind and type of IT and Network Infrastructure that you have.

- The combination of On-Prem and Cloud-based platforms that you have (this is also commonly referred to as a "Hybrid Environment").
- The total number of employees who will need Privileged Access.
- The kinds of employees that you have who will need Privileged Access, such as if they are regular employees or contractors (with the latter, as reviewed earlier in this chapter, will need to have extra safeguards embedded into the accounts).

There could be other factors as well, but the above list is the most common of them. Generally speaking, the following are the types of Privileged Accounts that exist today for most businesses:

1. *The Superuser Account*:
   This is also referred to as the "root", "admin", "administrator", or "supervisor" accounts. These kinds of Privileged Accounts grant specialized IT employees nearly unlimited privileges over any system that resides in the IT and Network Infrastructures. They allow for employees with these titles the ability to:
   - Execute commands.
   - Make system changes.
   - Create and modify files and settings.
   - Grant or revoke permissions for other users.
2. *The Domain Administrator Account*:
   Also referred to as the "domain admin", this is a Windows-based, Privileged Account that can edit information in the Active Directory (AD), the Azure Active Directory (AAD). They can do the following:
   - Create and/or delete users.
   - Assign, delete, and change user permissions.
3. *The Local Administrator Account*:
   Also known as a "local admin account", this allows for the user to access and make changes to a local Windows machine, which even includes wireless devices, and even Virtual Machines and Virtual Desktops which are set up in Microsoft Azure. However, this person with this kind of

account will lack the ability to modify information in the AD as well as the AAD.

4. *The SSH Keys*:
   The Secure Socket Shell (also known as the "SSH") keys are access credentials which provide direct root access to a Unix-like Operating System, such as that of Linux. This kind of access is very often done over a remote connection. This is typically used to implement Single Sign On solutions.

5. *The Emergency Account*:
   This is also called a "Break Glass Account". This allows for Network Administrators, Project Managers, CISOs, members of the IT Security team, and so on to bypass the access controls in a secure application in the event of a crisis, such as that of an Incident Response or even a Disaster Recovery in the advent of a security breach.

6. *The Privileged Business Users*:
   These are typically the employees who are non-IT related, such as those in finance, marketing, human resources, and other roles who may require Privileged Access to the sensitive systems.

Privileged Accounts for Machines

Believe it or not, it is not just humans who need to have Privileged Access Accounts. Given the digital world that we live in today, a lot of the repetitive tasks in the world of Cybersecurity are automated. This is especially true for Penetration Testing, Threat Hunting, and filtering out for false positives from all of the network security tools. The kinds of machines that would require a specialized type of Privileged Access account include those of Virtual Machines and Virtual Desktops that are set up in either AWS or Microsoft Azure.

The following are the types of Privileged Accounts that can be created for a machine:

1. *The Application Account*:
   Applications use these highly privileged accounts to access databases, run batch jobs or scripts, and confer access to other applications.

2. *The Service Account*:

Deemed to be among the highest risk Privileged Accounts, the Virtual Machines, and the Virtual Desktops that need these kinds of interactions with the Operating System can make changes and run scheduled tasks, all on an automated basis, with the help of the appropriate AI and ML tools.

3. *The AD Service Account*:

Also referred to as the "Domain Service Account", this type of account enables a Cloud-based or Web-based service to interact with an Operating System, manage users and computers, organize data, and change passwords, all on an automated basis using AI and ML tools.

4. *The SSH Key*:

Once again, automated processes through AI and ML tools can generate SSH keys to gain access to firewalls, routers, switches, and other sorts of network security devices.

5. *The Secret*:

Also referred to as "Privileged Credentials", these secrets include the following:

- API keys.
- Passwords (although the goal is not to use them as far as possible).
- SSH keys T.
- Tokens.
- Certificates which allow for both human and service accounts to securely authenticate to privileged systems.

How to Determine Who Gets PAM Privileges

By its very nature, one would assume first that anybody with a managerial or administrative title should be entitled to receive a PAM account if it is needed for their specific role. But it could be the case that a regular employee, or even very often, that a person needs to have access for just a very short time period. In this case, a concept called "Just-in-Time Access" can be used and will be covered in more detail later in this chapter.

First, it is very important to define what actually constitutes "Privileged Access". Here are three conditions in which this can be met:

- The granting and revoking access for other users.
- Connecting to and accessing sensitive data, such as Personal Identifiable Information (PII) datasets.
- The configuring and provisioning of a managed Cloud-based infrastructure, such as Microsoft Azure or AWS.

As you evaluate these three criteria, here are some other general tips to follow when you are provisioning PAM-based accounts:

1. Begin by defining roles for users and outlining required privileges and access rights for those roles. Remember to limit access by scope and time.
2. Second, give very serious consideration to which systems you would need to recover first in the event of an attack – those containing sensitive data, high-level permissions, and the ability to configure and access other systems.
3. Third, carefully review the access needs of third-party vendors, as it has been reviewed in detail earlier in this chapter.

The Security Risks Posed to PAM Solutions

Privileged Accounts is one of the primary objectives of the Cyberattacker. After all, once they have these kinds of credentials, they will have much quicker access to the proverbial crown jewels of your business. But this is not the only security that is posed to PAM-based solutions, whether they are based in the Cloud or On-Prem, or perhaps even both. The following is a sampling of what causes these other security risks to be born:

1. *Too much access*:
   There is no doubt any kind or type of restrictive Access Control can make the employee feel constrained, but it can also disrupt workflow and productivity. Because of this, overworked granting too much access will be granted. Obviously, this is one way that IT Security teams do not feel overburdened all of the time by having to assign, rights, privileges,

and permission all the time. But, worst yet, over-provisioned accounts are then forgotten or unmonitored, opening the door to a huge security risk.

2. *Privilege creep*:

When an employee changes roles within a company, they often retain access to systems they no longer need. As a result, the IT Security team will often add access based on the new or expanded role without revoking access to systems the employees no longer need and/or use. Without constant monitoring, these systems go unmanaged and may eventually be forgotten.

3. *Zombie accounts*:

Also referred to as "Orphaned" or "Abandoned" accounts, these result when an employee leaves the company for whatever reason and the privileged access is not disabled or deleted. Additionally, some accounts may be utilized less often until they become obsolete or forgotten.

4. *The unchanged defaults*:

PAM accounts, especially Service Accounts, often possess privileged access by default. Such applications, systems, and devices commonly ship with embedded credentials that are easy to guess and represent prime targets for the Cyberattacker.

5. *The static credentials*:

With On-Prem PAM-based solutions, the rotating and updating privileged credentials can be manually intensive and error prone. This results in default passwords that are never disabled and static passwords that are not rotated out or have no expiration date.

6. *The password sharing*:

Once again, although the goal of PAM is to get rid of passwords, when the same admin account manages multiple service accounts or IT teams share passwords across multiple systems, it becomes difficult to audit and manage privileged accounts.

7. *The lack of monitoring*:

The bottom line here is that you can't correct what you can't see. As a result, unmanaged privileged accounts may linger, becoming threat vectors that open the door to attack.

The Four Pillars of Privileged Access Management

Any PAM-based solution, whether it has been designed for the Cloud or an On-Prem Infrastructure, contains four distinct pillars. This is what makes the PAM solution work and can be considered as the primary engine. Here they are:

1. *The Managing of Access Privileges*:
   PAM allows businesses to prevent and respond to external and insider threats. It reduces the attack surface by establishing least privilege access for humans, processes, and applications, as well as the Virtual Machines and Virtual Desktops. This greatly diminishes the routes and entry points that a Cyberattacker can use to gain a foothold and limits the scope of damage should a security breach occur.

2. *The Centralizing of Administrative Access*:
   PAM takes a more holistic or macro approach to improving the workflows of employees. Without PAM, administrators may follow a different protocol for each system. With an effective PAM framework in place, the IT Security team can manage critical accounts from a central location. An added benefit is that employees can access the systems they need without having to remember multiple passwords. The bottom line is that this leads to greater productivity and reduced frustration.

3. *Privileged activity monitoring enhances visibility*:
   With privileged session management, the IT Security team and CISO can easily identify and respond to problems in real time. As a result, the activity of every privileged user – from employees to devices to third-party vendors – can be closely watched and monitored from beginning to end. Privileged session management improves more than just security. Also, a comprehensive PAM solution simplifies auditing and compliance requirements.

4. *The Privilege Management solution secures remote access*:
   Ever since COVID-19, distributed (also known as "Hybrid") and even fully remote workforces are becoming the norm. This simply means that more software-as-a-service (SaaS) applications, infrastructure automation tools, and service

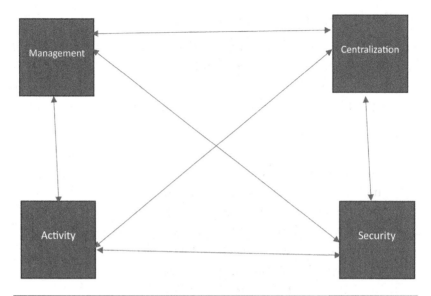

Figure 3.2   The Privileged Access Management (PAM) Model from the Standpoint of the Remote Workforce.

accounts are and will continue to connect from multiple locations.

These four pillars are illustrated in Figure 3.2.

As you can see from the diagram, all of these four pillars are interconnected with one another and any impact on one will have a cascading effect on the others.

Privileged Access Management versus Personal Identity Management

A Review of Privileged Access Management

The world of PAM is full of its techno jargon, just like Cybersecurity. In fact, there is a lot of confusion about what Privileged Access Management is versus Privileged Identity Management, also known as "PIM". Although we have covered in great detail so far in this book what PAM is all about, it would be useful once again at this stage what it is all about. Another technical definition of it is as follows:

PAM is what lets a user request the privileges needed for a specific system and be granted approval for their request so they can access it through their existing account. With PAM, administrators can grant a specific user privileged access to a single system for a set period of time. Usually, an administrator grants permission to the user for the length of time needed to complete the task that requires elevated permission, ranging from hours to days.

(Source: www.bravurasecurity.com/blog/the-difference-between-pam-and-pum).

So as you can see and what has been reviewed so far, in very simple terms, PAM is all about the methodology of granting the employees of businesses the higher level of privileges, rights, and permissions that they need to accomplish a certain task or project. These kinds of privileges are only given for the time period that is required, no more and no less. For example, if employee John Doe has been assigned to a software development team to help out with coding for a certain period of time, then the appropriate privileged access will be given just for that time period only. Once John Doe has completed his tasks for this project, these higher-level privileges will then be taken away, and his normal rights, privileges, and permissions will be reverted to what it was before.

A Review of Privileged Identity Management

In contrast, Privileged Identity Management, or "PIM", can be technically defined as follows:

In the PIM approach, privileged accounts are considered digital identities and not particular users or individuals, as is the case with PAM. In this sense, PIM and PUM are closely related since PUM deals with accounts, not users.

PIM lets systems administrators activate and deactivate roles based on timing and approvals. With more control over account activity, PIM lessens your organization's risk of users accessing sensitive resources when it's unnecessary, inappropriate or too frequent.

(Source: www.bravurasecurity.com/blog/the-difference-between-pam-and-pum)

Put in simpler terms, PIM is designed to assign privilege-based access to the roles that exist in a business entity. It does not deal with individuals directly. For example, the CISO and his or her IT Security team may decide to create a bucket called "Network Administrators" in Azure Active Directory (AAD). From here, they can then assign privileged access in an all-encompassing sense, and whoever fits or becomes this particular role will be automatically assigned these higher privileges.

But keep in mind that using the PIM approach requires much more careful attention than the PAM accounts. For example, the role and title of Network Administrator will always exist, unlike the PAM account, which is normally deprovisioned or discarded when it is no longer needed. Because of this, this has become the preferred method for assigning privileged-level rights and permissions.

Other Related Areas of Privileged Access Management

A Review of Privileged User Management   As it has been seen throughout this book, the methodology of PAM is to assign high-level privileges to users who need them or even create a specific account that the particular employee needs. In other words, there is only one account created for one user. As we have seen with Privileged Identity Management or "PIM", this is primarily used for assigning rights, privileges, and permissions for different job roles and titles; in other words, it is used to help create a "Digital Identity" that is secure.

But there are other methodologies that are related to PAM, and one of them is known as Privileged User Management, also referred to as "PUM". The technical definition of it is as follows:

> Privileged User Management (PUM) is the approach that limits or grants permissions based on the account type being accessed rather than the user accessing it. PUM refers to a system's built-in privilege accounts, such as a root or administrator account.
>
> (Source: www.bravurasecurity.com/blog/the-difference-between-pam-and-pum)

So, in other words, there could be one account which other employees need to access on a temporary basis. For example, assume that the

Database Administrator has their own PAM account. But it could also be the case that other members of the IT Department also need access to this account, such as the Network Administrator, and perhaps members of the IT Security team may also need access as well.

So, in this particular instance, both of these groups will be given very restricted access to the Database Administrator to do the jobs that they need to do. Once this part is over, then their rights, privileges, and permissions will be deprovisioned. Another option would be to create a clone of the Database Administrator account and assign the needed privileges from that. Then once the work is done from the Network Administrator and IT Security sides, this cloned account can then be deleted. A key advantage of using this account is that there will be no interference or cross-over to the "real" Database Administrator account.

A Review of Cloud Infrastructure Entitlement Management

Entitlements merely refer to the rights, privileges, and permissions that are assigned to a PAM-based account. In any CIEM model, there are typically four main components, which are as follows:

- Entitlement Visibility.
- Rightsizing Permissions.
- Advanced Analytics.
- Compliance.

To start the process, once an entitlement has been defined, the CIEM platform will then assess it to determine whether the access privileges it grants are the least necessary for achieving a workload's intended purpose, following the concept of Least Privilege. If there is too much access, an alert is then triggered to the administrators so that they can address the problem manually. The CIEM platform can also adjust entitlements automatically, which allows teams to work efficiently in large-scale environments.

It is important to keep in mind that rather than using generic rules and conditions, the CIEM platform relies heavily upon advanced analytics powered by both Artificial Intelligence (AI) and Machine Learning (ML). Also, User and Entity Behavior Analytics (UEBA) are used quite a bit as well. The CIEM platform can also detect periods of "drift" in which entitlements that were once compliant fall out of it as a result of configuration changes. The end goal of CIEM is to have a more secure platform for enforcing least-privileged access credentials across Cloud resources and providers.

A good and highly reliable CIEM platform will consist of the following characteristics:

- A deep visibility into the rights, permissions, and privileges that have been assigned to resources in your Cloud-based PAM accounts.
- A governance platform for the monitoring of excess and unused PAM accounts based in the Cloud. The goal here is to reduce "PAM Sprawl" as much as possible.
- An automated and responsive framework that automatically adjusts PAM-based permissions, rights, and privileges – and takes actions in case of misalignment.

There are also six strategic benefits to using a CIEM platform in the Cloud, and they are as follows:

1. *Deep visibility into entitlements*:
   This allows the CISO to gain a complete view of identities, policies, and access risks across multi-Cloud environments and platforms.
2. *Enhanced Identity and Access Management*:
   According to Gartner, more than 95% of accounts in IaaS use less than 3% of the entitlements they are granted. Many companies have inactive identities from former employees. CIEM solutions continuously monitor access activity to identify outdated identities and, from there, disable them.
3. *The automation of detection and remediation*:
   By using both AI and ML, the CIEM platform can calculate the baseline profiles and, from there, detect events like account compromise, insider threats, stolen access keys, and other potentially malicious user activities.
4. *Audit-ready*:
   Along with other tools available from AWS or Microsoft Azure, the monitoring and securing of entitlements across

your Cloud platforms will allow for your organization to adhere to compliance regulations and standards related to user permissions.

5. *Specialized for SaaS solutions*:
   The CIEM solution offers specialized, identity-centric SaaS solutions focused on managing Cloud access risk via administration–time controls for the governance of entitlements.

6. *Does a deeper dive*:
   The CIEM toolset expands deeper into Identity Controls (like Governance of Entitlements and Identity Analytics and PAM and IGA Process Integrations)

Once all is said and done, the complete CIEM platform will look something like Figure 3.3:

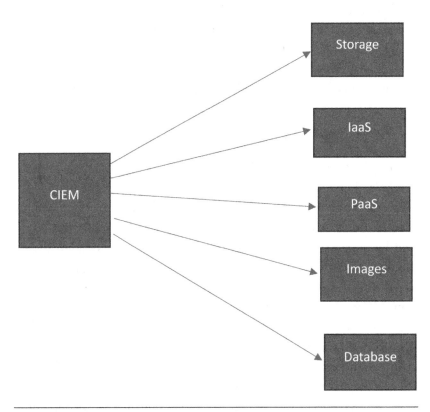

Figure 3.3   The CIEM Model.

A Review of Just-in-Time Access

Another closely tied component of Privileged Access Management is what is known as "Just-in-Time Access", also known as "JIT" for short. A technical definition of this is as follows:

> Using the just-in-time (JIT) access methodology, organizations can give elevated human and non-human users in real-time to provide elevated and granular elevated privileged access to an application or system to perform a necessary task. Cybersecurity industry analysts recommend JIT access as a way of provisioning secure privileged access by minimizing standing access.
>
> JIT access helps organizations provision access so that users only have the privileges to access privileged accounts and resources when they need it, and not otherwise any other times. Instead of granting always-on (or standing) access (or standing access), organizations can use JIT access to limit access to a specific resource for a specific timeframe. This granular approach mitigates the risk of privileged account abuse by significantly reducing the amount of time a Cyberattacker or malicious insider has to gain access to privileged accounts before moving laterally through a system and gaining unauthorized access to sensitive data.
>
> (Source: www.cyberark.com/what-is/just-in-time-access/)

In simpler terms, this can be compared to a supply chain/logistics example. For example, a production line will not want to hold an excess amount of inventory to build the products on the assembly line. Not only will it take critical space in the warehouse, but it will also be quite expensive to hold all of those raw materials until they are needed. So what most companies today have adopted is what is known as the "Just-in-Time Inventory". This is where all of the raw supplies are ordered right before the production process is about to begin. Or, a retail store may order enough products "Just-in-Time" to keep up with the fluctuations in demand from their customers.

The same can be said of "Just-in-Time Access" as it relates to PAM. The IT Security team will give only elevated rights, permissions, and privileges just as they are needed in time by the employee who is requesting them. Then once the work or project is done, those privileges are then deprovisioned. In this regard, there are three main types of Just-in-Time Access accounts, and they are as follows:

1. *The Broker and Remove Access*:
   This approach enables the creation of policies that require users to provide a justification for connecting to a specific target for a defined period of time.
2. *The Ephemeral Accounts*:
   These are one-time-use accounts, which are created at the right moment that they are needed and immediately deprovisioned or deleted after use.
3. *The Temporary Elevation*:
   This method allows the temporary elevation of privileges, enabling users to access privileged accounts or run privileged commands on an as-needed request basis. Access is then deprovisioned when the time period is up or the rights, privileges, and permissions are no longer needed.

Although deploying the Just-in-Time approach will vary from business to business, the following is the general methodology that is followed:

1. A human or non-human (such as a Virtual Machine or Virtual Desktop) requests privileged access to a server or a central repository where shared resources are stored.
2. The request is then verified against a pre-approval policy or is reviewed by an administrator who has the power to grant or deny the request for short-term privileged access. It is import that this particular process can be automated by making use of AI and ML.
3. Once approval has been granted, the human or Virtual Machine or Virtual Desktop can then access the system and perform their specified task. This access can last for only a few minutes or for a few months, which is dependent upon the following criteria:
   • The user's specific task(s).
   • The organization's governance and security policies.
4. After the task or project has been completed, the access is then revoked or deleted until it is needed again.

This process is illustrated in Figure 3.4.

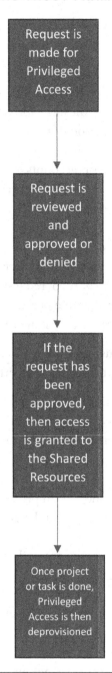

Figure 3.4 The Just-in-Time (JIT) Approach.

Using "Just-in-Time Access" for Privileged Access Management has a number of strategic advantages, which are as follows:

1. It helps businesses improve their overall Cybersecurity posture by significantly reducing the risk of privileged access abuse.
2. It helps ease and simplify the administrator/IT Security team by removing the need for review cycles.
3. It helps improve compliance with the various data privacy laws, such as those of the GDPR, CCPA, and HIPAA. Another benefit is that this process greatly simplifies PAM administration by minimizing the number of privileged users and privileged sessions and having full audit trails of all privileged activities.
4. Just-in-Time Access for PAM also allows for the attack surface of a business to be greatly reduced, by getting rid of the "standing" PAM accounts that remain idle and unused for a long period of time.

For more detailed about Just-in-Time Access for PAM, click on the following link: http://cyberresources.solutions/ZTF_PAM_Book/JIT_PAM_WP.pdf

The Security Issues Privileged Access Management "Sprawl"

Now that we have covered in a good amount of detail the major components of PAM, as well as some of the security issues that go along with them. In this section of this chapter, we look at some of the issues that the Cloud infrastructure entitlement management can pose to a PAM-based solution that also exists in the Cloud, whether it is the AWS, Microsoft Azure, or even the Google Cloud Platform. As of now, the biggest threat in this area is the overissuing of both PAM-based accounts and even the assigning of too many rights, privileges, and permissions.

Take these statistics into consideration:

- The AWS: 98% of PAM permissions are not used as they have been assigned.
- The Microsoft Azure: 98% of PAM permissions are not used as they have been assigned.
- The Google Cloud Platform: 95% of PAM permissions are not used as they have been assigned.

- It is estimated that, by next year (2024), there will be well over 2,300 violations of PAM-based policies on these major Cloud platforms.

(Source: The CloudKnox and Gartner Reports of 2021)

As it was alluded to earlier in this chapter, overprovisioning PAM accounts can lead to very serious problems, especially when it comes to a security breach. For example, by having so many accounts, you are merely expanding the attack surface for the Cyberattacker to penetrate. Once in, not only will they have direct access to the super user accounts, but, from this, they can wreak total havoc across all of your Cloud-based platforms, with a worst-case scenario being a total wipe out of your Virtual Machines, Virtual Desktops, and most importantly, all of the information and data that you have about your customers. In turn, this will put your business into the cross hairs of regulatory auditors, with the potential of facing huge fines.

Of course, all of this could have been avoided if more attention had been paid to deprovisioning those PAM accounts when the work was done (for which they were needed) or no longer being used. To help avoid PAM Sprawl, here are three techniques that your business should consider implementing:

1. *Identity Consolidation*:
   As it was just described, this refers technically to the discarding and replacement of existing Identity Management Systems (also known as the "IMS"), which is namely the PAM solution. While this may seem to be the obvious and quick way forward, there can be consequences if it is done in a haphazard fashion, and not planned properly ahead of time. The CISO and the IT Security team need to do a careful review of the original purpose behind the system's initial deployment in the first place. For example, a very important to consider is: was the PAM solution deployed because it offered a Multifactor Authentication (MFA) or because it also offered highly resilient directory services that could integrate with the AAD? It is important to keep in mind that discarding such features could be an expensive step backward as such features will need to be replaced by another tool. Or, worse yet, this could even require a costly reworking of unsupported applications and services.

2. *Identity Orchestration*:

   A newer approach is what is known as "Identity Orchestration". This adds an abstraction layer that applications can use to integrate with other Identity Systems without having to alter any application or source code. This kind of approach replicates identities and policies retrieving identity from other various identity stores.

3. *IAM Centralization*:

   IAM is an acronym that stands for "Identity and Access Management", and, in fact, Privileged Access Management is considered to be a subset of it. With the Centralization approach, the primary goal is to get PAM Sprawl under control by centralizing the identities of all users, devices, and applications. This can be achieved by creating global profiles of every identity and cross-checking the attributes and privileges across every source of identity data. This is to ensure that privileges match their roles.

Where Privileged Access Management Sprawl Exists – The IaaS

As has been mentioned in this chapter, the IaaS is an acronym that stands for "Infrastructure as a Service". A technical definition for it is as follows:

> Infrastructure as a service (IaaS) is a type of Cloud computing service that offers essential compute, storage, and networking resources on demand, on a pay-as-you-go basis. IaaS is one of the four types of Cloud services, along with software as a service (SaaS), platform as a service (PaaS), and serverless.
>
> (Source: https://azure.microsoft.com/en-us/resources/
> cloud-computing-dictionary/what-is-iaas)

Put in simpler terms, this is the portion of the Cloud that provides all of the critical resources, tools, and services that are needed to completely build out your deployment. Because of just how important the IaaS is, this is also where the most number of Privileged Access Management accounts reside. As a result, this is the one area in which most PAM sprawl exists. In this regard, there are three types of entitlements that can be used at this particular level in the Cloud, and they are as follows:

1. *The Resource Entitlements*:
   These can be considered as the rights, privileges, and permissions that are assigned to control the core components of the IaaS. These include primarily File Storage, Virtual Machines, and the Virtual Databases, along with the Virtual Desktops.

2. *The Service Entitlements*:
   These can be viewed as the rights, privileges, and permissions that are assigned to maintain (or "service") the core components of the IaaS. These include primarily File Storage, Virtual Machines, and the Virtual Databases, along with the Virtual Desktops.

3. *The Management Entitlements*:
   These can be thought of as the rights, privileges, and permissions that are assigned to keep command (or "govern") the core components of the IaaS. These include primarily File Storage, Virtual Machines, and the Virtual Databases, along with the Virtual Desktops.

The CISO and their respective IT Security team should consider seriously using any and/or all of the strategies to reduce PAM Sprawl at the level of the IaaS.

Various Issues of Privileged Access Management in the Cloud

Despite the apparent advantages that a Cloud-based PAM has over the On-Premises PAM, there are still some issues with it that need to be reviewed. They are as follows:

1. *Constant Monitoring*:
   Given the nature of privileged access, one of the optimal routes to take is to have constant monitoring of the accounts that have been created and are in use. Although no human being can feasibly do this, this is where the automated tools of AI and ML can come into play. While theoretically they can be run non-stop on a real-time basis, one still has to ensure that the relevant information and data are being fed

into them. This also takes human intervention to make sure that the datasets are cleansed and optimized.

2. *The Instances and Workloads*:

It is a given fact that today Cloud deployments are expanding rapidly, and this is causing a huge uptick in the total number of Instances and Workloads that are being created on a daily basis. Because of this, more PAM accounts have to be created at an almost exponential rate, thus resulting in the "Sprawl Effect" reviewed earlier in this chapter.

3. *Serverless Access*:

The term "Serverless" has been used quite a bit recently, but what does it exactly mean? Here is a technical definition of it:

> Serverless refers to a Cloud-native development model in Cloud computing that allows developers to build and run applications and services without needing to manage infrastructure or server-side IT. Applications in the serverless model rely on a combination of managed Cloud services and functions as a service (FaaS) that abstract away the need to manage, patch, and secure infrastructure and virtual machines.

Put in simpler terms, if you are a software developer and run on a software development team, your main job is to create the application and not worry about anything else. So with a Serverless environment, you need not worry at all about that; the entire infrastructure is provided and managed for you. In a way, it is just like having your very own Platform as a Service (PaaS). But, when it comes to PAM, the main issue here is that the "Just-in-Time" provisioning cannot be used here.

4. *The Use of APIs*:

Many software development teams often make use of APIs to cut down on development time. Essentially, these are libraries of code that can be used over and over again and even customized to meet the needs of the development project. But APIs can also pose a grave security risk, and, because of that, a PAM solution will be needed here as well. But, unfortunately, when it comes to security for software development, this is often an overlooked area. So if PAM accounts were to be deployed to the software developers that need them, there is a good chance that these accounts will also be "forgotten" about and not deprovisioned in time.

5. *The Databases*:

The primary engine that fuels your Cloud deployment is the Virtual Databases that you provision. After all, they contain the datasets that are the lifeblood of your company. Because of this, anyone who needs access to them will need to have so-called Super User Privileges. These are the highest levels of rights and permissions that can be assigned to an employee. Of course, you will obviously need to establish PAM accounts for these individuals, and if they are not governed and deprovisioned in a timely manner, a Cyberattacker can easily get access to and hijack these particular accounts and rain down entire havoc on your entire business.

6. *The Use of DevOps*:

DevOps can be technically defined as follows:

> DevOps is a combination of software development (dev) and operations (ops). It is defined as a software engineering methodology which aims to integrate the work of development teams and operations teams by facilitating a culture of collaboration and shared responsibility.

(Source: https://about.gitlab.com/topics/devops/)

While a PAM-based solution would be needed here for sure, the main problem here is that it would be difficult to change the mindset of the software development and operations teams to actually adopt, because at the present time, it does not technically fall under the guidance of Identity and Access Governance policies.

What Businesses Really Need

So far in this chapter, we have reviewed in detail the components and strategic advantages of what Privileged Access Management offers to a business. But what is it really that CISOs (even vCISOs) and their IT Security teams aspire for in such a solution? Here are four main areas:

1. *Broad Visibility*:

Have a 24 × 7 × 365 holistic view of the access and activity of all employees and digital assets, across all business and financial transactions, and have the ability to monitor all of the Cloud infrastructures, workloads, data archiving, storage, and processing.

2. *Active Risk Intelligence*:
   The real-time detection of evolving threat variants in any kind of environment with integrated usage analytics that can be queried for at any time.

3. *Granular Enforcement*:
   Ensuring that appropriate access at all times is strictly enforced and that the concept of Least Privilege is also deployed and audited on a regular basis.

4. *Security Enabling Business*:
   To enforce continuous review without inducing user fatigue, especially for the IT Security team. This also means using automation through AI and ML to filter the false positives from PAM-based alerts and warnings.

So, to crystallize all of this together, the best combination for any business is to have a PAM-based solution that is deployed into the Cloud, across all deployments and infrastructures. This will also include the Cloud Infrastructure Entitlement Management (CIEM) and Just-in-Time (JIT) Access platforms. Here are the major highlights of how this combination would work:

- The real-time monitors of all of the Cloud-based platforms to make sure that there is no abuse of the entitlements that have been assigned.
- The constant usage of Audit Logs to send alerts, warnings, and messages to an SIEM console for intervention by the CISO and IT Security team. Again, a primary objective here is to greatly reduce the total number of false positives that get into the SIEM.
- To have built-in, fine-grained governance across anything that exists in your Cloud-based deployment.
- To make Entitlement and Privileged clearly defined in the security policies and also as part of the upfront onboarding process a top priority.
- To greatly reduce the attack surface by deploying Just-in-Time Access.
- Constantly enforce the concept of Least Privilege for every right and permission that is assigned to employees.

The Battle between On-Premises and Cloud-Based
Privileged Access Management

Even despite the fact that a Cloud-based PAM solution provides far
more strategic value to an organization than an On-Prem PAM solution,
businesses are still creatures of habit and, in many cases, are still quite
hesitant to make the full migration. Figure 3.5 depicts this scenario:

Figure 3.5   The Disadvantages of an on Premises Privileged Access Management (PAM) Model.

The Best Practices for a Privileged Access Management Cloud Deployment

We have covered a lot about Privileged Access Management, but now it is very important to review some of the guiding principles or the best practices when it comes to deploying it. Although this list focuses primarily on implementation into the Cloud (such as the AWS or Microsoft Azure), it can be also used to varying degrees for an On-Prem PAM solution as well. So, here is what you should be doing to get the most out of your PAM solution:

1. *Write a formal security policy for your PAM solution*:
   As a CISO, it is very important to create a formal policy not only for your PAM solution but also for all of the Privileged accounts that you provision. Thus, it is crucial that you look at the privileged account types as well. Some key questions you need to consider:
   * Which of these PAM Accounts do you have in your organization?
   * Which employees need access to them and for how long?
   * Is it possible to segment networks and systems to make it easier to contain a security breach? In other words, can you deploy the Zero Trust Framework with a PAM solution implemented into it?
2. *Change or remove Embedded Credentials:*
   The technical definition of an Embedded Credential is as follows:

   Hardcoded passwords, also often referred to as embedded credentials, are plain text passwords or other secrets in source code. Password hardcoding refers to the practice of embedding plain text (non-encrypted) passwords and other secrets (SSH Keys, DevOps secrets, etc.) into the source code. Default, hardcoded passwords may be used across many of the same devices, applications, systems, which helps simplify set up at scale, but at the same time, poses considerable cybersecurity risk.

   (Source: www.beyondtrust.com/resources/glossary/
   hardcoded-embedded-passwords#:~:text=Hardcoded
   %20passwords%2C%20also%20often%20referred,
   into%20the%20source%20code)

Thus, it is very important to change or remove embedded credentials, default IDs, and passwords for Privileged Service Accounts.

3. *Educate your workforce:*
   We have all heard about the importance of Security Awareness training for employees, but now it is more crucial than ever before, especially when it comes to PAM Accounts. Explain in great detail the importance of rotating out credentials on a regular basis, implement Multifactor Authentication (MFA), and use SSO (especially Biometrics) to totally eradicate the need and use for passwords.

4. *Enforce the principle of Least Privilege:*
   This is a topic that has been greatly discussed in this book thus far. As a CISO, it is very important that you and your IT Security team strictly enforce and make your employees adhere to the concept of Least Privilege for both human and machine accounts (these include Virtual Machines and Virtual Desktops). Restrict account creation and permission levels to the exact resources a person or system needs to fulfill a defined role, no more and no less.

5. *Inventory Cloud applications, SaaS accounts, and other third-party systems:*
   As it was stated before, this is where the importance of conducting a Risk Assessment comes into play. This is really the only venue where you will know for sure what you have (from both a digital and physical asset standpoint and just how vulnerable they are). Enforce extremely strict PAM policies for both internal and external resources. Pay extremely close attention to the way contractors and third-party vendors access your network, and make sure that you have an exhaustive vetting process in place.

6. *Vault, rotate, and manage secrets:*
   Here, it is very important to vault, rotate, and manage secrets for the Privileged Accounts that you create and provision, for anywhere they are deployed, whether in the Cloud or On-Prem. You need to pay very careful attention to Privileged Accounts associated with Containerization Services, Machine Learning Environments, and Infrastructure Platforms that you make use of for any kind of Cloud deployment.

7. *Monitor, audit, and analyze Privileged Session Activity:*
Increase visibility into your network so you can detect and correct catastrophic user errors and malicious activity before the problem spreads. This is where you need AI, ML, and a SIEM console the most. The good news is that the major Cloud providers have this available, at no extra cost to you.

8. *Revisit your policies on a regular basis:*
Just as important as it is to review, rehearse, and update your Incident Response, Disaster Recovery, and Business Continuity Plans, the same holds true for your PAM solution. IT is very important that you revisit your policies on a regular basis and, ensure that your best practices are updated on a regular basis.

9. *Planning for Privileged Access Management at the Enterprise Platform Level:*
Businesses find it to be efficient to centralize the responsibility for the management of their servers and databases into one internal infrastructure into one IT Security team rather than several "Stove-Piped" teams spread around the business. Having a centralized approach encourages consistency in the deployments and configurations of these resources. But, at the same time, it can also increase the risk of Privileged Access violations as administrators now can have it across an entire enterprise rather than just within an individual business unit.

    A successful PAM program needs to understand these potential risks by classifying the types of agents that exist within the enterprise, the breadth of their access, the processes used to manage the Privileged Accounts, and the impact of the accounts that should be compromised.

10. *Planning for Privileged Access Management at the Application Level:*
How Privileged Access will be granted, revoked, and monitored should be done as early as possible in the first phase of the Software Development Lifecycle (SDLC). But, this is most needed in the maintenance phase for the applications that have been created. In this regard, extensive redevelopment and sometimes complete re-engineering of the

application could be needed if Privileged Access Controls are applied too late in the SDLC process.

11. *Deploy Control Selection and Layering*:
    For this to happen, consider the value of the information Privileged Access Users will have access to. If the risk of a breach is too high, additional technical or operational controls can be added, such as more frequent activity monitoring, use of a rights management system, or even file-level encryption.

12. *Deploy an Account Provisioning process*:
    It is important to note that whenever you provision a brand-new PAM Account, whether it is done by a human or even a machine (using AI and ML), you need to have a defined process to make sure no errors, intentional or not, are mitigated as much as possible. Here is a process that you can follow:
    - The Privileged Access Roles must be clearly defined at both the platform and application levels to help ascertain the appropriate privileges, rights, and permissions for those employees who need this kind of access. The roles should clearly align with major functions within the system.
    - A centralized authority should be notified of all new user requests and provide an approval sun process for those requests. This is necessary to ensure all requests are properly vetted and are a key artifact for auditors governing the PAM process of your business.
    - The employees should be assigned only to appropriate roles, adhering to the concept of Least Privilege. If that person's privileges need to change, they should be moved to the role that grants those privileges only, and any old accounts should be deprovisioned immediately.
    - Users and system managers should be required to review access privileges and attest to the need for Privileged Access so that unnecessary access does not linger and accumulate.

13. *The Management of Production Code Promotion*:
    The Production Promotion is the process of moving changes to an application or software into the operational environment.

This is a huge source for assigning Privileged Access to all web-based applications that have been created. For example, a software developer does their source code creation in an offline mode, typically in a Test Environment. Once the process starts of moving this to a Production Environment, the software development team will require the highest level of privileged access. Very careful attention needs to be paid here, as the risk of Insider Threats is quite high. For example, a disgruntled employee could build logic bombs or backdoors, build processes that quietly steal information, or even fraudulently delete, alter, or modify any datasets that have been used to build out the web application.

Thus, it is also very important to fully ensure that software developers and their corresponding teams do not retain their level of privileged access in the production environment under any type or kind of condition. As an extra layer of security, source code reviews should also be conducted to specifically target the "service hooks" (also known as the "Backdoors") which software developers often use to legitimately modularly test the source code that they create.

The bottom line is that the software developer who initiated the change through Privileged Access should not be the same person who promotes this code in the Production Environment.

14. *Always be Auditing*:

It is crucial that you do this on a regular basis, and stick to your schedule. Here is a process that you can follow:

- Review a random sample of Privileged Access Authorizations: Gather the access request forms/tickets that were submitted to gain Privileged Access.
- Review all access to Critical Infrastructure, especially your Cloud-based Deployments: It is crucial that key servers and network devices get a full access review to ensure all employees have appropriate permissions, rights, and privileges.
- Review a sample of Privileged Access to Non-Critical Infrastructure: This involves auditing every other digital and physical asset in your IT and Network Infrastructures.

15. *Make your employees accountable for their credentials*:
    Eliminate Privileged Access sharing by holding your employees responsible and accountable for all of the Privileged Accounts that they have been assigned. This can further reduce the risk of what is known as "Credential Sharing".

16. *Implement the Separation of Duties*:
    Beyond implementing the principle of Least Privilege, the Separation of Duties is key for every identity that needs access to Privileged Systems. Preventing this requires defining roles and tasks across an environment so that users have separate credentials across different account types. In technical terms, Separation of Duties can be defined as follows:

    > Separation of Duties is the means by which no one person has sole control over the lifespan of a transaction.

    (Source: www.fa.ufl.edu/directives/
separation-of-duties-overview/)

17. *Continuously monitor Anomalous Behavior on Privileged Accounts*:
    This is one of the most basic, cardinal rules in all of Cybersecurity. In this regard, you will want to make use of what is known as "Session Recording". This helps IT Security teams monitor activity across hundreds or thousands of Privileged Account Sessions. Any action that occurs outside that baseline sends an alert to security teams and offers an easy way to prioritize and monitor unusual actions. No human being has all the time in the world to do this, so make sure you deploy a PAM-based solution that incorporates AI and ML to automate this process and filter out for the false positives.

18. *Deploy Attribute-Based Access Control*:
    Attribute-based Access Control (also known as "ABAC"), gives a mechanism to businesses with a new way to establish even firmer command over the users' behavior of their Privileged Access Account. ABAC incorporates two more dimensions to a Privileged Access Account: to the mix: the taken actions and the environment in which they were transacted. Important to note here:

- Actions: This defines what the user is trying to do with the resource, such as Read, Write, Edit, Modify, and Delete.
- Environment: This speaks to the broader context of where the resource is being used, including time and date, location, the device itself, and any supporting protocols.

The Weakness of Repeated Authorization and Authentication

The second major weakness of the traditional Zero Trust Framework is its repeated need to keep authenticating and authorizing an end user (or an employee) each and every time they need to get access to something. Although the philosophy of the Zero Trust Framework is to "never trust" but keep verifying, it can really be a nuisance in the end. On top of that, having to go through this process over and over, especially for larger companies, can tax computing and processing.

Not only that, the end users (or employees) can also get frustrated with having to go through this process every single time. Is there a solution for this? Yes, and the answer resides in what is known as "Privileged Access Management". In a very broad sense, this area deals with providing a higher level of security for those accounts that are deemed to be a higher level than the regular employees. For example, this includes the likes of the CISO, network administrator, Database Administrator, or even the project manager on a software development team.

Essentially, anybody who has a managerial at the IT level will have these kinds of accounts. A technical definition of Privileged Access Management (also known as "PAM") is as follows:

In an enterprise environment, "privileged access" is a term used to designate special access or abilities above and beyond that of a standard user. Privileged access allows organizations to secure their infrastructure and applications, run business efficiently and maintain the confidentiality of sensitive data and critical infrastructure.

Privileged access can be associated with human users as well as non-human users such as applications and machine identities.

As one can see from this definition, even AI and ML can be given a Privileged-Level Access. It is important to note at this point that all of the authorization and authentication information and data are kept in what is known as a "Secret Vault". This is where the automation process comes into play. For example, if a network administrator needs to gain access to a server, all he or she has to do is simply click on the application icon, and they will be automatically logged into the server.

The login credentials to this server are already stored in the Secret Vault. The network administrator will have their Privileged Account, and the rights and privileges for the server will be stored here. So, when this individual clicks on the application icon on their desktop or wireless device, this will trigger a response to be sent from the Privileged Account to the Secret Vault, requesting that access be made to this particular server. From here, the Secret Vault will then transmit the login information to this server, and, within seconds, the network administrator will be able to get into the server.

This is illustrated in Figure 3.6.

This same approach can also be used for the Biometric Templates, and this will be discussed later in this chapter. But since PAM is such an integral component of our proposed Zero Trust Framework, it is necessary to do a deeper dive into it, to gain a much firmer understanding of it. The next few sections will get into more detail.

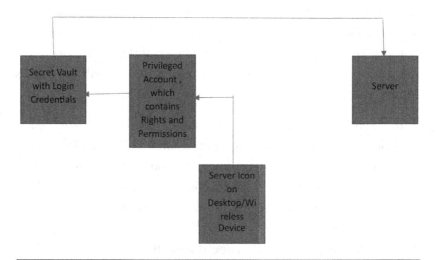

Figure 3.6   The Secret Vault in a Privileged Access Management (PAM) Model.

The Strains of On-Prem PAM

Before the COVID-19 pandemic hit, mostly all businesses had an On-Prem Infrastructure, or some parts of it were also located on a Cloud-based platform, such as that of AWS or Microsoft Azure. But using PAM in this manner is now showing it is not viable for the following reasons:

- The IT and Network Infrastructures of today are no longer deemed to be static. Rather, they are dynamic, with many end users logging in at the same time to access shared resources, as well as the sheer influx of information that businesses have to store today in data warehouses, and the various states that they have to go through. These include if they are archived, are transmitted to different points, or are being processed and analyzed.
- Access to the above often made use of GUIs to access a PAM server to get the privileged login information. This was done all manually, thus adding more administrative headaches to an already strained process.
- Logging into separate applications required multiple logins into the PAM server to access the proper credentials. Given today's mantra for automation and APIs, and as a result, this is no longer feasible to use.

PAM-based solutions are much better suited for Cloud-based deployments, especially when it comes to the Hybrid Cloud, as the next section examines.

Why PAM Is Better Suited for the Cloud

As companies today make the full, 100% move to a Cloud-based environment, PAM will be far better suited here for this kind of environment, for the following reasons:

1. *Direct access is now a reality*:
   In today's world, not only do software developers want quick access to their code, but they also now have to follow the rules of DevSecOps. Having a tool such as AD not only provides a secure way to give out privileged access but the same login credentials can be used over and over again on

different development tools until the so-called Time To Live request has expired. In this case, the software developer will then have to go back to AD to get a new set of privileged credentials.

2. *You can keep existing workflows*:
   It is a basic fact that humans are sheer creatures of habit. We don't want to change unless we absolutely have to. This is especially true of software developers. Once they have become accustomed to a certain way of creating source code and the tools that are used to compile it, they don't ever want to adopt a newer way of doing things. But using PAM in the Cloud allows for what is known as "Native Tooling". This allows for the software developers to keep using the tools that they have become accustomed to for so long while adding in richer layers of authentication protocols.

3. *You can make use of the latest code development practices*:
   DevSecOps not only embraces the automation process but also allows PAM to support the following functionalities in the Cloud:
   - *Promote the usage of Infrastructure as a Code*:
     This is simply the provisioning and management of your Cloud infrastructure through the use of a certain programming language, rather than using the old-fashioned, manual processes. This enhances the speed of automation, and helps to cut down on the number of security-related mistakes that occur in the source code creation process.
   - *Configuration as a Code*:
     This allows for an automated version control system to be deployed in your Cloud infrastructure. Through this, you will have increased states of visibility, automated Quality Assurance (QA) testing, and ways to revert back to older editions of the source code, if the need ever arises to do so.

4. *It can help to support the various ChatOps tools*:
   The Remote Workforce of today is heavily reliant upon the use of various Instant Messaging (IM) tools now more than ever before. Examples of these include platforms such

as Slack and Microsoft Teams. Integrating PAM here, such as Just-in-Time (JIT) requests, allows for privileged access provisioning and approval to happen a lot quicker and more efficiently than doing this on an On-Premises infrastructure.

5. *It will help to create a Passwordless environment*:
Let's face it, the password has been the de facto standard for both authentication and authorization purposes, and while it is expected to do so, a PAM solution that has been built for the Cloud will help to totally eradicate the need for passwords. This is so because many organizations are now making their best efforts to go to a Passwordless system, such as using tokens, digital certificates, and Biometrics.

6. *It will support diverse kinds of operating environments*:
Although the movement now is to have PAM support gaining access to administrative credentials that are based in the Cloud (such as that of Azure), a workable solution will also support a Hybrid environment where credentials can be granted securely where a company makes use of a Cloud and On-Prem environment. This is so because not all companies have chosen yet to make the full migration to the Cloud, some still prefer to have part of their infrastructure based on Prem.

The Advantages of Using PAM in the Cloud

Obviously, deploying a PAM-based solution in the Cloud is far better than using On-Prem. The benefits can be detailed as follows:

1. *Centrally store and manage passwords*:
In today's business world, passwords are among the biggest nemesis that is faced. For example, the cost to reset a password is pegged to be about $100.00 per employee. If you are a smaller SMB, this may not come to a lot of money in the end. But if you are a Fortune 100 company with thousands of employees worldwide dispersed globally, this cost can add up quickly and take a toll on the bottom line. Sure, there are other tools you can use out there, such as the basic

Password Manager. However, there are inherent security flaws with those as well, especially when it comes to overseeing those employees who have privileged access accounts. What makes PAM unique in this sense is that it brings to the Cloud a high-powered "Password Vault", which allows to you manage and assign administrative privileges from a single dashboard, in a very safe and secure environment. Nobody else but you will be involved in this process unless you have other IT Managers that you want to grant this kind of access to.

2. *Easier to enforce the Concept of Least Privilege*:
   One of the cardinal rules in Cybersecurity is to give employees just enough access to shared resources for them to do their job on a daily basis. Although this sounds simple in concept, enforcing it and keeping what employees have is another story. For example, the IT Security team may give out admin-level credentials for a contractor only for the time that they are at your business. Once they are done with their work, this account should be immediately disabled, but many times it gets forgotten about. Or employees may share their passwords behind your back. Whatever the situation is, you need a tool that can oversee and execute the concept of Least Privilege on a real-time basis. This is where PAM will play a crucial role. Once deployed in a Cloud environment, it can automatically assign privileges on a needed basis, following the rules and permutations that you have set forth. But, best of all, it will terminate those accounts which no longer need those privileges for certain applications. In other words, you don't have to go through every computer and wireless device to make sure that the baseline rights and permissions have been assigned and/or deleted. The PAM can store all of the employee profiles, and decide when to allocate and disable permissions automatically. This reduces the risk of forgotten accounts still being activated, which could create a potential backdoor for a Cyberattacker. This is also known as "Just-in-Time Access" and can even be used for members of the IT

Security team to reduce the probability of misuse of admin-level privileges.

3. *Control Remote Access*:

   With the COVID-10 pandemic still upon us to varying degrees, the Remote Workforce is here to stay permanently. While many of the initial security issues were worked out when WFH was first launched a couple of years ago, many of the traditional security tools have been stretched beyond their breaking points. A prime example of this is the Virtual Private Network (VPN). Before the pandemic hit, it did an excellent job of encrypting and securing the network lines of communications. But this was when only 15%–20% of all employees were working from home, not the near 100% capacity we are seeing now. Thus, the Cyberattacker now has greater ease with which to penetrate the VPN, gain access to privileged credentials, and even hijack a remote session. But, by implementing a PAM solution into your Cloud environment, you can make use of the Zero Trust Framework and implement what is known as the "Next Generation Firewall", which far surpasses the security thresholds that are offered by the VPN. Not only will this prevent the hijacking of privileged access credentials, but you will have logging activity recorded on a real-time basis, which makes auditing far easier and simpler.

4. *Protecting interconnectedness*:

   As the digital world is coming together, so are the objects that we interact with on a daily basis, which include those in the physical and virtual worlds. This is technically known as the "Internet of Things" or the "IoT". The Cloud has also made a great extent these objects to interact with one another, but the problem is that the end users still have the security set to the default level, which also includes making use of a very weak password. When PAM is implemented into the IoT infrastructure you have deployed into the Cloud, it can manage the creation and assignment of appropriate privileges to the end users on an automatic basis. It will even assign passwords that are far more robust than what a traditional Password Manager can create.

5. *Secure DevSecOps in the Cloud*:

This was a concept that was introduced in the last article. This is a merging of three distinct teams:

- Software development;
- Operations;
- IT Security.

One of the central themes of DevSecOps is automation. While PAM can be used here once to protect privileged access to the source code, it can even do much more than that, for example:

- Secure developer accounts.
- Secure Encryption Keys.
- IT Security.

One of the central themes of DevSecOps is automation. While PAM can be used here once to protect privileged access to the source code, it can even do much more than that, for example:

- Secure developer accounts.
- Secure Encryption Keys.
- Secure Digital Certificates.

A Best Practices Guide for Deploying a PAM-Based Solution

Just deploying the Zero Trust Framework, deploying a PAM-based solution takes careful planning and testing before releasing it into the Production Environment. Here are a few tips to help ensure a smoother deployment:

1. *Understand why you need PAM in the first place*:

You simply should not deploy a PAM solution just because you think you need to. You first need to think carefully about why you need one in the first place, and if you decide to have one, then you need to map very carefully how it will fit into your IT and Network Infrastructure. You need to fully ascertain which systems, processes, and technologies will be requiring this. Then you need to figure out who will have access to the PAM solution these are keys to the proverbial crown jewels of your organization.

2. *Create a PAM password policy*:

   You should already have a password policy in place, but the one for PAM will be different in the sense that you need to craft it so that it addresses the needs of those who have managerial or IT admin titles. Having such a policy in place will help to avoid any misuse of credentials, as Cyberattackers love to go after these kinds of passwords. Therefore, it is recommended that you follow the guidelines from entities such as SANS, NIST, and ISO. Remember to change out passwords on a regular basis, and, just like for your regular employees, they should be made long and complex and just a little bit more, as these credentials will give access to the most sensitive areas of your business. Also, make sure you implement Multifactor Authentication (MFA) to make sure 100% that only legitimate employees have access to privileged accounts. Some of these second and third layers of authentication can include the use of passphrases, RSA tokens, Smart Cards, and Biometrics.

3. *Change out default passwords*:

   Once you have created a privileged account, make sure that the person to whom it is assigned immediately changes the password. Even though the default password may be long and complex, it is always a good practice to make sure it is changed out when the account is first activated. Make sure you put into your PAM security policy what these passwords need to contain. This will be an alphanumeric string, but what detail it needs to contain needs to spell out to avoid any confusion or mistakes. Remember, your employees do not have to create these kinds of passwords. The PAM functionality should take care of all of this on an automatic basis. But it is always a clever idea to conduct an audit from time to time as to who has what access when it comes to privileged accounts.

4. *Keep tabs as to what is going on*:

   Just as much as the IT Security team has its eye on the Cyber Threat landscape, you also need to keep an eye on what is happening to the privileged accounts that you assigned. For example, you need to make sure that those employees who have these kinds of accounts are abiding by every letter of the PAM password policy. Of course, you will not be able to keep track of all of this on a 24 × 7 × 365 basis, so this is where you can use the tools of both Artificial Intelligence (AI) and Machine Learning (ML). They can keep an eye on you on these accounts on a real-time basis and alert you in case there is any type of anomalous or suspicious behavior that is transpiring. Keeping track of all this will give you the essential metrics that other members of the C-Suite will ask for and even the Board of Directors. Keeping track of this will also be very advantageous to you in case you are ever faced with an audit by regulators from the GDPR, CCPA, HIPAA, and so on.

5. *Make use of Least Privilege:*

This was reviewed in one of the previous articles. With this, you are assigning the minimal amount of permissions that are necessary for your employees to conduct their daily job tasks. But this holds true also for those employees who have privileged accounts. Just because they are technically at a higher plane because of the level of access, you still need to follow the concept of Least Privilege here as well. For instance, you would grant your IT Security Manager access to all of the devices in your company, so that they can install the needed software patches and upgrades, and perform other troubleshooting tasks. For your Network Administrator, you would assign those rights and permissions that are needed to gain access to the network, the servers, etc. These are privileges that your IT Security Manager would not need, and vice versa.

6. *Deletion of temporary accounts:*

At times, it may be necessary for you to set up a privileged account for an outside third party, especially if you hire a vCISO. Rather than assigning an original, privileged account for them, create a cloned account, and from there, you can then specifically configure the privileged access this individual will need, based upon their contractual obligations to you. Set this account to be inactive on their last day. This way, you will not have to worry about forgetting this task, it will be done automatically for you.

The Mistakes That Are Made When Deploying PAM Solutions and How to Fix Them

Even despite the care that you and your IT Security take, mistakes are always inevitable. Here is the common list of mistakes made and how to correct them:

1. *How up to date are your systems?*
   The PAM solutions of today are mostly compatible with the latest technologies. For example, deploying a solution for Windows 10 will not work for Windows 8, as it is a much more out-of-date system. Before you deploy a PAM configuration, it is very important to make sure that it will work with all of the digital assets in your business. The best way to do this is to take an inventory of all of the hard wired and wireless devices that you have. If anything is outdated, then it is time to discard and upgrade ASAP. This is not just from the standpoint of launching PAM, but it is a rule of thumb in Cybersecurity that any outdated device can pose a serious risk, as this is one of the first items that the Cyberattacker will go after.

2. *Not applying passwords properly*:
   This has been a widespread problem for decades, and it is only getting worse. Many employees are given admin passwords, whether it is intentional or not. By doing this, they will be able to log in to the most sensitive areas of your business and cause any type of havoc, such as data leakages. Or worst yet, they can accidentally give out these passwords to a Cyberattacker in a Social Engineering attack. Password sharing still remains a huge problem as well, and this is one of the leading causes of Insider Attacks to precipitate. To avoid all of these problems, you need to separate the normal everyday employees from those who are eligible to have

privileged access. The former group should have its own set of security policies, whereas the latter should have its own as well. While both should be enforced equally, the group of employees with the privileged access need to have further scrutinization. In other words, you don't want to have password misuse here, as the effects can be far more serious. You are dealing with privileged accounts. To make sure that all is airtight, it is imperative that you check for any types of suspicious behavior on these types of accounts. This can include multiple login attempts that have failed, or trying to login to a resource to which they have no business in doing so. You can keep a daily watch on all of this by implementing AI tools, and having any alerts or warnings transmitted to the SIEM, where a dedicated member of the IT Security team can proactively triage them.

3. *Create the right kinds of profiles in AD*:
   One of the primary benefits of AD is that you can create as many user groups as you need, and from there, assign privileges on an ad hoc basis. For example, you can create a user group for all of the accountants that work in your company, and import into that all of the individual usernames. From there, you can create all of the privileges for that profile, and deploy all of the privileges and permissions in a simultaneous fashion. While this is certainly advantageous, it can also prove to be a serious mistake from the standpoint of the privileged user groups. You do not want a help desk specialist to have network administration privileges assigned to them by accident. So in this manner, you are probably better off assigning rights and privileges to privileged accounts manually, rather than on an ad hoc basis. True, this will take more time, but at least you will have confidence that the appropriate permissions have been applied. This is where having a separate list created for the privileged accounts will be very useful, as described earlier in this article.

4. *The move to the Cloud*:
   The movement to the Cloud is now happening at a pace than it was ever imagined. A lot of this has been fueled by the

COVID-19 pandemic, and in this rush, security is now a forgotten topic. When you move all of your applications to the Cloud, you need to take an inventory of what you have just moved, and from there, determine which of those assets need the highest level of protection. Of course, you will need some sort of PAM architecture here, but this too will need to be protected as well. In other words, you simply cannot assign privileged accounts and merely trust your IT Security team will not run off with them. There could be a malicious threat actor here as well. Therefore, you will even need to keep a careful eye here, because, in today's world, you simply cannot trust anybody anymore, even those employees that have been around for a long time. In other words, the days of having implicit trust even in the most minute degree are now over, it is time for the Zero Trust Framework.

5. *Outside vendors*:

As the world becomes more interconnected partly fueled by the IoT revolution, businesses are becoming more dependent now upon hiring third-party contractors to help meet customer demands and expectations. It is highly recommended these days that you have a deep vetting process in place before you make a selection. But this is where most companies make their mistake. They don't continually monitor the hired third party after the fact. It is very important that you do audits on a regular basis, to confirm that there are no leakages of your datasets and that all privileged accounts that have been assigned are not being misused in any way.

The Importance of Just-in-Time (JIT) Access

In the world of supply chain management, there is a concept known as "Just-in-Time Inventory". This is when the raw inputs are delivered to the manufacturer right before they are needed to complete the final product. The idea here is to eliminate excess inventory in an effort to cut unnecessary costs. This is also somewhat similar to JIT Access, but instead, it deals with the establishment of the rights, privileges, and permissions that are needed in a privileged account and is assigned to a specific role right when it is needed the most.

To illustrate this example, take the role of the Project Manager who is overseeing a software development team. This group is developing a web-based application for a client, and the Project Manager needs to gain superuser network access to see how the prototype product will work on both the front and back ends of a server.

To accomplish this, the IT Security team will provide JIT Access that is designed specifically for the role of a Network Administrator. During this time, the Project Manager will then see how the protype runs, and make any notes of tweaks and adjustments that need to be made to the source code. Once this task is over, the IT Security team will then completely disable the JIT Access until it is needed again for a similar situation.

This example illustrates what JIT Access is and from the standpoint of a specific role. In a company, there can be accounts that are established for specific privileged roles, with all of the rights and permissions that go with them. So when is absolutely needed, it can be activated, and once the work is done, it can be disabled, or deactivated once again.

The basic idea of JIT Access is to avoid keeping privileged access accounts in an always "on mode", which can be a huge risk from the standpoint of Cybersecurity. It is also based upon the principle of "Least Privilege", which states that only the minimal rights and permissions should be given, even in the case of superuser accounts, like PAM.

The Four Pillars to PAM Success

The top four major components that the CISO and his or her IT Security team need to examine are as follows:

1. *Track every account*:
   A privileged account is one which has some superuser privileges to a certain degree. These credentials could involve things such as database administration, network administration, and security administration. Therefore, these kinds of accounts need to be safeguarded very carefully and constantly

monitored. After all, if a Cyberattacker can gain access to just one Privileged Account, then the chances are much greater that they will be able to move laterally in a quick manner to your digital assets. Therefore, any good PAM solution should have the functionality to keep track of each and every account that has been, even if it is for just a few hours. Also, the solution must be capable of either deleting or deprovisioning any inactive PAM-based accounts. Also, information about the use of Privileged Accounts needs to be collected which will form your governance strategy as to how they will be given out in the future.

2. *The limiting of Access Control*:
   There are two characteristics of Privileged Accounts that you need to be aware of: (1) Access Control; and (2) Access Governance. With the former, you need to keep track of all of the changes that are made from the Privileged Accounts itself. For example, these accounts can be regarded to be dynamic in nature. The profiles and the groups in these accounts will change over time, depending largely on how the security policy of your organization changes. Thus, the IT Security team must keep track of these changes. If there are too many of them being made from the established baseline, then this could be a cause for concern. With the latter, you need to keep track of what Privileged Accounts can access. You do not want any cross-over between the entitlements that have been established for a network administrator to have database privileges. In other words, a Privileged Account should only give access to what is urgently needed for just a brief period of time.

3. *Record activity*:
   Any good PAM-based solution must give the CISO and the IT Security team the ability to capture the activity of all of the Privileged Accounts on a real-time basis. The reason for this is that this data will prove to be extremely valuable when it comes down to doing an internal audit, or even one that may be conducted by federal regulators. However, parsing through all of this data can be a very burdensome

task and can even prove to be an administrative nightmare. Thus, the PAM-based solution must have the ability to give a visual representation of all of the information that is being collected. Moreover, it should also have the functionality for the IT Security team to build specific queries not only to extract data but also to examine what-if scenarios down the road.

4. *Automation*:

    In today's world, the IT Security team is inundated by threat vectors on a minute-by-minute basis. Although constantly Privileged Accounts are of a high priority, it cannot be done by a human being; it is just too much to ask for. Therefore, any PAM-based solution must have automation built into for the following, to just name a few:

    • Doing mundane and repeatable tasks.
    • Establishing configuration changes.
    • Conducting software upgrades and patch maintenance.
    • Service shutdowns and startups.
    • Event log management.
    • The establishment of Multifactor Authentication.

The Finer Points of Privileged Access Management

As you deploy the Zero Trust Framework for your organization, keep these granular details in mind as well:

1. *Privileged Access Governance*:

    We all know that most organizations have higher-level accounts than the rest of the employee base. These are the Privileged Accounts, and these are typically assigned to those employees that have some sort of administrative role, such as a network or even a database manager. Even a project manager on a web development project could very well be assigned a privileged account so they can oversee the project from beginning to end. Although the goal of a PAM-based solution is to properly govern these accounts when they are needed and not needed, they do not observe how the privileged end user actually interacts with the sensitive data to which they have access. For example, are there any malicious activities that are transpiring? Are these privileged accounts being abused in any way? This is where the Privileged Access Governance component comes into play. From this, in a single view, you can see any signs of abnormal behavior toward the data. There are log files that are provided for this very reason, so you will be able to get any first indicators of an insider attack that could be brewing. This comes all under the umbrella of what is known as "User Behavior Analysis". The Privileged Access Governance functionality can also draw out various visual diagrams as to where all of your sensitive datasets reside. This is especially useful to have to come into compliance with various data privacy laws.

2. *PAM Discovery*:

   If the organization is especially large (starting at a 1,000-employee size or greater), Privileged Accounts can be created and used without even the IT Security team knowing about it. The primary reason for this is that it is the job of the IT department to do all of this. Very often, there is a lack of communication between both parties, and, quite often, one party does not know what the other is doing (and vice versa). Therefore, you need some sort of functionality in your PAM-based solution to keep any Privileged Accounts that are being created and onboarded. This is where the PAM Discovery component will come into use. Scans can be triggered automatically, and messages sent to the IT Security team whenever a brand-new Privileged Account has been initiated and onboarded. This functionality will also give you the ability to keep a continuous eye on those Privileged Accounts and recycle those that are outdated into a newer state with updated rights, privileges, and permissions.

3. *Privileged Credential Management*:

   This can also be referred to as "Privileged Password Management". However, this is not to be confused with that of a Password Manager. This refers to just the creation and storage of passwords for the everyday consumer, who has many passwords to remember. The Privileged Credential Management component of a PAM-based solution keeps track of those login credentials that are strictly associated with Privileged Accounts. Technically, it can be specifically defined as follows:

> It is the secure storing, sharing, creating, and handling of privileged passwords. Privileged password management may alternatively be referred to as privileged credential management, enterprise password management, enterprise password management, enterprise password security. Privileged passwords are a subset of credentials that provide elevated access and permissions across accounts, applications, and systems.
>
> (Source: www.beyondtrust.com/resources/glossary/ privileged-password-management)

As can be seen from this definition, privileged passwords are just one part of all of the passwords that are established for all of the other employees of a company. But it is considered to be a subset, given the special characteristics that they have. But passwords are only a set of credentials that can be used with PAM-based solutions. These include tokens and SSH keys.

Because of the sensitivity that is involved with credentials associated with PAM accounts, they have to be monitored in a much different way than other password management techniques. In this regard, some of the best practices include the following:

- Keeping a constant eye on these kinds of credentials.
- On a 110% level, privileged credentials must be rotated on a regular basis per the security policies that have been established.
- Bring all of the privileged credentials into one central location, which is known as the "Vault".
- Keep an on malicious behavior that can impact any PAM-based credential. This should be an automated basis, which will most likely make use of AI and ML plug-ins to comb through all of the log files.

Privileged Session Management

This component of a PAM-based solution is meant to serve as a system of checks and balances. For example, if a network administrator logs in using a Privileged Account, then he or she can be observed on a real-time basis by the IT Security team from the moment they log in, when they are in session, and when they log out. The primary objective here is that somebody else with the same privileges can keep an audit trail by another person who also has the same types and kinds of privileges. This can also serve to be very advantageous for compliance reasons.

Privileged Access Management in the Cloud

As this chapter has reviewed so far, there are many advantages that a Cloud-based platform offers over an On-Premises setup. But, while they still continue to be advantages, they are now a must-have for any business if they are to make the leap into digital innovation. Being in the Cloud, whether it is the AWS or Microsoft Azure is now a priority for the following reasons:

- Retaining and capturing more of the market share.
- Maintaining a strong posture and competitive advantage to garner new customers.
- The ability to greatly reduce both administrative and infrastructure overhead and expenses.
- Speed up your marketing process for new products and services.
- Allow for the "anytime, anywhere" access for both your employees and clients, even new ones.

To summarize, these are some of the key advantages that a Cloud infrastructure offers to any business, no matter what industry they might be serving:

- It is scalable and elastic, which simply means that resources are ephemeral (which means that they only last for a short time, because there are so many other new SaaS-based apps that are coming out).

- Overall, the Cloud is a borderless computing ecosystem in which geographic bounds are not realized. This simply means that distributed workforces can access resources from anywhere and at any time.
- No matter what Cloud environment you are using (such as AWS or Azure), it is built for speed and agility. But this in turn can lead to security gaps, such as data leakages, whether they are intentional or not.
- Cloud environment applications communicate with one another on a real-time basis, between the IaaS, the SaaS, and the PaaS.

But, despite these strategic benefits as just examined, Cloud computing ecosystems can become very complex very quickly, which means that new systems and processes will be needed to make sure that they are intact from the standpoint of security. It is anticipated that this complexity is only going to get worse as businesses go toward hybrid and/or multi-Cloud environments, which also bring in on-premises systems. This greatly exacerbates the challenges of maintaining visibility and control for any kind of deployment or infrastructure.

Because of all of these interconnections, perimeter-based defenses are no longer valid. Instead, *Identity is now what matters the most, especially when it comes to the Zero Trust Framework and PAM.*

The Limitations of Traditional PAM Models in the Cloud

As it has been described in previous chapters, PAM is needed greatly to protect those accounts that are deemed to be "super user" or "high level" in general. Some examples of these include accounts that are created for the network administrators, the database administrators, the IT Security team, and even some employees from the IT department. Even the rights, privileges, and permissions that the CISO can be considered to be privileged as well.

But the problem here is that the traditional PAM-based models, while they may have worked for the On-Premises infrastructures, simply do not work for today's modern, Cloud deployments. The following reasons are cited for this:

- The traditional PAM technologies typically handle privileged accounts by storing administrative accounts' credentials in a password vault. From here, the appropriate rights and permissions are allocated. But they are not time or task-limited. Rather, they have "standing privilege". This simply means that anyone who has privileged access to resources has it for an unlimited amount of time, with no checks or audits being performed.

- As a security precaution, PAM solutions can scan environments at pre-assigned intervals. However, they were not designed to suit the dynamic nature of Cloud environments where new virtual machines and other resources are spun up and scaled down in a matter of just a few minutes.

- Traditional PAM solutions were created to handle traditional user accounts with the username and password being the main login credentials. Because of this, many lack the capabilities needed to handle items such as the IoT, the Industrial Internet of Things (IIoT), Robotic Process Automation (RPA), or CI/CD pipelines.

- A bulk of the PAM vendors offer control solutions that get deployed to the endpoint agents. This is a much more macro-based approach in that it provides privileged access by focusing on applications instead of individual users, who have specific PAM accounts. Because of the advances in the Cloud, this archaic approach is quickly becoming obsolete.

- Additionally, in legacy environments, users requiring privileged access to applications would often be provided with two accounts: standard access and privileged. This worked well with the perpetual licensing models widely used for on-premises applications but adds unnecessary licensing costs for SaaS offerings that are priced according to their total number of users.

- Legacy PAM also introduces additional complexity into the process of identity lifecycle management. It makes it relatively easy for orphaned accounts – belonging to terminated employees or other former users – to persist in the environment for long periods without monitoring or oversight. Furthermore, legacy PAM solutions cannot cope with the fine-grained nature of role assignments and permission sets in SaaS applications.

- Because of the huge demands based on SaaS apps, legacy PAM tools are cumbersome to manage, even in 100%, pure on-premises infrastructures.
- The legacy PAM models are also not suited to the modern ways of doing business. In today's world, it is increasingly common for third parties to require privileged access to an organization's data and systems, causing a security peril.

Because of these aforementioned issues with the legacy PAM-based solutions, there is now a seismic shift to create PAM solutions that are devoted to just Cloud-based platforms, with support for an On-Premises infrastructure if the business chooses to maintain this kind of hybrid approach. In fact, the major PAM vendors are now offering their solutions as a SaaS offering.

For example, CyberArk now makes their primary PAM solution available in the Marketplace for Microsoft Azure. With just a few clicks of the mouse, the administrator of that account can deploy the entire solution in just a matter of a few minutes. Some of the advantages that PAM-based Cloud solution brings to the table are as follows:

- Cloud-based PAM solutions automate simple decision-making about whether or not to grant particular access requests. Anything more complicated than this is automatically to IT Security for a more thorough review.
- Errors are eliminated while saving time and reducing management complexity.
- Cloud-based PAM solutions can seamlessly integrate risk-based business intelligence into approval workflows.
- Cloud-based PAM solutions integrate with both DevOps and DevSecOps tools.
- As previously stated in this book, it also integrates very well with Security Information and Event Management (SIEM)

platforms and other security alerting infrastructures. It can also work with other types of Identity Governance solutions.

- Because PAM-based Cloud solutions are Cloud based, there is no need to invest in infrastructure. Any configuration is done for you.
- Cloud-based PAM solutions offer ways to manage privileged accounts to minimize vulnerabilities and limit the potential for damage if compromise occurs.

Conclusions

The overall benefits of a PAM-based Cloud solution are listed in Table 3.1.

Table 3.1 The Overall Benefits of a PAM Cloud Solution

- It provides a central console in which the IT Security team can view all events. This is done via the SIEM.
- It can be used for various kinds of instances and workloads, whether the development environment is Linux or Windows based.
- It can support serverless functions, such as CI/CD pipelines.
- It can protect APIs and view all of the rights, permissions, and privileges that are assigned to the software development team.
- It can govern all sorts of databases that are provisioned in the Cloud, whether they are SQL or non-SQL based.
- It can support the use of Command Line Interfaces (CLIs, such as that of Power Shell) for both DevOps and DevSecOps purposes.

4

THE PASSWORDLESS SOCIETY

Introduction

As it was alluded to in great detail throughout this book, one of the primary goals of both the Zero Trust Framework and Privileged Access is to not only enforce Multifactor Authentication (MFA) but also, as much as possible, try to get rid of the usage of passwords altogether. As we all know, passwords can be extremely pesky, especially if you have to abide by company policy to create long and complex passwords.

But passwords have been around for quite some time, and the unfortunate part about this is that they will continue to be so, for a long time to come. This is even despite the fact that there are a number of other viable solutions that are available, such as the use of Biometric technologies as reviewed earlier in this book. Some of the most robust modalities that one can use in this regard are Fingerprint Recognition, Facial Recognition, and Iris Recognition. There are other Biometric-based modalities that a business can use, but they don't have a wide-reaching market, at least as of yet.

But before we delve further into why passwords should be removed entirely, it is important to review at this point what their inherent weaknesses are:

1. *Passwords are not friendly*:
   This is actually a double-edged sword. When it comes to accessing your personal information and data, you obviously have a lot of freedom to choose the passwords that you want to use. For example, many people create very simple passwords (even using the word "password"), or they use the same password over and over again, even for multiple applications, which makes that a very risky situation. But now at your place of employment, it is quite likely that your employer is going to mandate that you create a long and complex password, which

 DOI: 10.1201/9781003470021-4

can be almost impossible to remember. Thus the temptation to write them down and make them visible in plain sight poses even much greater security challenge.

2. *Technically, passwords are not secure*:

   Once again, this is yet another Catch-22. For the longest period of time, it has been ingrained into our minds that passwords are the only true means to keep our identity secure, but, as this book has reviewed, this is far from the truth. For example, passwords can be:

   • Easily shared with other co-workers, family, or friends.

   • From the standpoint of the Cyberattacker, they can be easily stolen or hijacked, especially if they are not encrypted.

3. *Passwords that have terrible entropy*:

   In this regard, the term "entropy" means what the password syntax actually contains. Here are some poor practices that people use which make them such a huge security risk:

   • The recommended minimum of characters is at least eight. But many people use much shorter amounts.

   • To fully remember the password, many people use numbers but in a sequential fashion. For example, back to our previous example: instead of just using "password", it is recommended that you have a series of numbers of alphanumeric characters like this: "password1!2@3#". But instead, "password123" becomes the top choice.

   • To attempt to create a stronger password, people will try to use a pattern on the keyboard that they are familiar with. But the problem here is that if their device gets hit with a Trojan Horse or any other type of malicious payload, a key logger can be installed and can quite easily and covertly detect this pattern.

   • To keep a password memorable and also in an attempt to make them sort of complex, people will try to use the names of family or friends in them. While this could work for some time, if the Cyberattacker launches what is known as "Dictionary Attack", from there, the password can be easily guessed.

4. *Encryption is not used*:
   This is essentially where any information and date are con-
   verted into a garbled format, which will not make sense to
   anybody. This process is known as "Encryption". The only
   way to render the content into a decipherable format is to
   follow a process known as "Decryption". But to both of these
   processes in any flow, you need to have the appropriate key,
   which would be either Public or Private. But many companies, especially the Small- to Medium-Sized Businesses
   (SMBs) don't follow this protocol, and, instead, the passwords of employees are sent in a clear, Plaintext fashion. This
   simply means that the particular password is as clear as day
   to anybody in both the internal and external environments.
   Thus, even creating a long and complex password serves no
   purpose unless it is fully encrypted.

5. *Passwords are inherently not safe*:
   One of the greatest security vulnerabilities of using passwords is that people simply do not store them in a safe place.
   While it is understandable that people will still have the urge
   to write them down, they should be kept somewhere where
   they are hidden from plain view. In fact, this phenomenon
   has become what is known as the "Post-It Syndrome", where
   employees of a business will write down their passwords on
   a Post-It Note, and stick it with tape to their workstation
   monitor.

6. *Need to change them all the time*:
   Today, businesses are realizing the constant need to keep
   rotating out old passwords and creating brand-new ones
   from scratch. While this will create a good security policy
   in terms of password protection, it is a huge irritant to the
   employees. Although they will have to abode by the rules
   and regulations that you have set forth, the truth of the
   matter is that ultimately they will try to find a way to circumvent it. There is always the option to use what is known
   as a "Password Manager". This is simply a software pack-
   age that can create, store and rotate out long and complex
   passwords. But the conundrum here is that this requires a
   password in of itself.

7. *Consider this*:
   - 62.9% of people change their password only when prompted.
   - 45.7% of people reuse a password for multiple sites/applications.
   - 52.9% of people share their password with colleagues, friends, and family members.
   - 67.1% of people believe that managing passwords for multiple accounts is not a waste of time.
   - 35.7% of people still jot down their passwords on paper, or sticky notes, or use planners.
   - 30% of the users have experienced security breaches due to weak passwords.
   - 88.6% of the surveyees use two-factor authentication.
   - 57.1% of the respondents say they use "show password" option only sometimes.

8. *Other reasons*:
   The following are also reasons that have been cited which cause employees to circumvent creating a stronger password and, instead, use something that is very weak, thus posing a grave security vulnerability:
   - Not being able to use the same password for logging into different applications.
   - Passwords now have to meet stringent syntax requirements, such as having the password be at least 16 characters long, with a mixture of lower/uppercase letters, numbers, and other forms of alphanumeric characters.
   - Losing the ability to write down passwords and putting them in an area that is insecure.
   - Passwords have to be reset on a regular basis, such as at least every 3 months. The new password can bear absolutely no resemblance whatsoever to the old password, thus making the new one even harder to remember.
   - Passwords cannot be shared with other co-workers, even third-party suppliers.
   - Passwords cannot even be shared with other members of the same project management team.

(Source: www.goodfirms.co/resources/top-password-strengths-and-vulnerabilities)

The next subsection of this chapter will review in more detail how the components of the Zero Trust Framework can help lead to the proverbial "Passwordless Society".

The Components of a Passwordless Society in the Zero Trust Framework

The basic mantra of the Zero Trust Framework is to "Never Trust, Always Verify". In simpler terms, any sort of trust, even in the least amount, cannot exist at all. Given this hypothesis, even the employees who have been with you the longest simply cannot be trusted. Everybody must have their identity confirmed over and over again if they are to gain legitimate access to shared resources. Although 2FA can work well here, the preference is to use MFA, where at least three or more layers of authenticating mechanisms can be used.

But the key here to remember is that to make the Zero Trust Framework, you have to deploy those authentication mechanisms that are different from each other. For example, one layer could be a challenge/response question, one could be an RSA token, and the other could be a Biometric modality of sorts. It will defeat the purpose of the Zero Trust Framework if you have two authentication mechanisms that are the same, such as two RSA Tokens because in a rapid-fire, sequential fashion.

Although the concepts of the Zero Trust Framework have been reviewed in detail at the beginning of this book, there are six main pillars to it, which will help lead to a passwordless society. They are as follows:

1. *The Zero Trust Identity*:
   This is deemed to be the crux of the Zero Trust Framework, as this is where the mantra of "Never Trust, Always Fire" resides. Also, the concept of Least Privilege resides here as well. The point of this is that no matter who the employee is, you should only give them just enough rights, privileges, and permissions to do their job on a daily basis, and no more.
2. *The Zero Trust Networking*:
   This states that the IT and Network Infrastructure of any business must be segmented into different zones or

islands. Each one of them must be separated with its own means of layered authentication, preferably using that of MFA. The main intention of this is that with so many layers in the Zero Trust Framework being present, it should be statistically impossible for the Cyberattacker to break through all of them and gain access to the digital assets. With this part of the Zero Trust Framework, there can be no network connection between the servers that hosts the shared resources that the employee is requesting access to. Before these specific network connections can be established, the end user must be fully authenticated by using an MFA approach. In this aspect, any Zero Trust Methodology places a heavy emphasis upon protect of the Endpoints, which still poses a huge source of risk for many businesses today.

3. *The Zero Knowledge Authentication*:
   Although the theme of constant verification is plausible in theory, realistically it is probably not feasible to do. The reason for this is that it would be time consuming and laborious, but employees could get literally frustrated with this in the end. So to alleviate this to some degree, this component of the Zero Trust Framework was also added. Essentially, another external party (called the "prover") can vouch for the identity of the individual to the authority that will be granted access to the shared resources (called the "verifier"). In return, any personal details of the individual are not revealed. As data privacy becomes of paramount importance today, this is another way for businesses to not have to store any type of PII dataset in their own IT and Network Infrastructure.

4. *The Zero Trust Passwords*:
   This is part of the Zero Trust Framework that addresses the elimination of the usage of passwords. To achieve this objective, "device identification with location, context, Biometrics, and device certificates delivers a more effective and efficient model". (Source: Zero Passwords in a Zero Trust World, a Tech Vision Whitepaper, published on 1/28/2020).

5. *The Zero Trust Provisioning*:

   This component of the Zero Trust Framework advocated that any Privileged Access account should be provisioned automatically when needed, and immediately deprovisioned when it is no longer needed. This saves time for the IT Security team to do this, and if this were to be done on a manual basis, it would often be forgotten about, thus leading to a grave security risk.

6. *The Zero Trust false positives*:

   The Zero Trust Framework highly advocates the usage of both Artificial Intelligence (AI) and Machine Learning (ML) to eradicate the issue of false positives filtering into the system. It also is a proponent of the use of SIEM-based technology.

Apart from the recent adoption by businesses for the Zero Trust Framework, there are other key variables as well which are also prime catalysts for the advent of the "Passwordless Society". These are as follows:

1. *The rise of Multifactor Authentication*:

   The first attempt to replace passwords was done by using Two Factor Authentication, also known as "2FA". This is where just two layers of authentication are used to confirm the identity of an individual. However, many businesses started to use passwords as one of these mechanisms, thus defeating the purpose of having it all together. Because of this flaw, there is now a much stronger movement toward using MFA, even if a business does not fully deploy the Zero Trust Framework.

2. *The rise of Privileged Access Management*:

   Privileged login credentials have always been a much-sought-after target of the Cyberattacker. Because, with one shot, they can gain access to the crown jewels of any kind of business. But with PAM, the goal here is to get rid of passwords and to use other identifying markers of an individual, such as Biometrics.

3. *The rise of Contextual Awareness*:

This concept is technically defined as follows:

> Context awareness is the ability of a system or system component to gather information about its environment at any given time and adapt behaviors accordingly. Contextual or context-aware computing uses software and hardware to automatically collect and analyze data to guide responses.
>
> Context includes any information that's relevant to a given entity, such as a person, a device, or an application. As such, contextual information falls into a wide range of categories including time, location, device, identity, user, role, privilege level, activity, task, process, and nearby devices/users.

Put in simpler terms, the primary objective of Contextual Awareness is to ascertain the kind of environment from which the employee is requesting access to shared resources from and use objects from the external environment as forms of confirming the identity of him or her. A good Identity and Governance Management will help to support this. Both AI and ML can be used to extract the right kinds of datasets based on this.

4. *The rise of Self Sovereign Identity*:

This is where the use of Decentralized Tokens will come into play. It can be technically defined as follows:

> A decentralized application (dApp) token coordinates activity for applications running on top of blockchains that provide services such as trading and lending, data storage, and even publishing blogs. They can be used to pay for access, reward users for utilizing a service, or let holders participate in governance and strategy decisions.
>
> (Source: www.forbes.com/sites/digital-assets/article/ what-are-dapp-tokens/#:~:text=A%20decentralized% 20application%20(dApp)%20token,storage%2C% 20and%20even%20publishing%20blogs)

When compared to the first three alternatives, this one would be more complex and resource intensive to deploy, as it would require the use of the Blockchain.

The Origins of a Passwordless Society

Believe it or not, the concept of eradicating passwords altogether started about 20 years ago, through a standard that was defined by IEEE P1363.

IEEE P1363 – Wikipedia

This standard gave rise to what would become known as the "Zero Knowledge Password Proof". This is where one party can prove to the other party the identity of the employee in question. This is done by sharing the hashed value of the password, and not the password itself. Using this specific technique greatly reduces the risk of any entity from properly guessing the password.

Key Considerations for the Passwordless Society in a Zero Trust Framework

Before a business embarks on this journey, there are a number of key considerations to take into account, and these are as follows:

1. *The User Experience*:
   This will rely on how easy it is for users to move to a new way of authentication. To make this transition easier, users should be allowed to authenticate themselves using options they are familiar with, for example, PIN, fingerprint scan, and facial recognition. But not using passwords! There will be a learning curve and training will be needed to use Biometrics and newer technologies.
2. *The Levels of Security*:
   The recovery process in the case of malfunction, loss, or replacement of a device should be well-crafted, designed and made as secure as possible. It should not result in reliance on legacy recovery methods that could expose users to credential-based attacks. It is important to stay up to date on new attack

vectors and having a proactive mitigation framework/plan in place is absolutely crucial. Additionally, periodic security reviews to review the overall security posture must be considered in the overall risk management processes and procedures.

3. *The Technologies That Are Involved*:
The businesses' application landscape, both On-Premise and Cloud, should be evaluated to understand if they support passwordless authentication, for example, a review of password-based legacy applications. It is also possible that modern applications may not support it in their base versions or may require additional costs to enable a passwordless society.

The Key Stakeholders in the Passwordless Society

It is also important to keep in mind the key parties that will be involved in this new journey, and they are as follows:

1. *The Remote Workforce*:
Deploying passwordless authentication will help reduce friction, enable remote work, and eradicate helpdesk password reset costs. In this instance, platform authenticators are best suited for a workforce that has dedicated laptops or desktops, whether they work remotely or in an office setting or not. Further, roaming authenticators can be deployed for a workforce that shares machines Mobile phones as a roaming authenticator can enable Corporate America to phase out hard tokens typically used for secure remote login, privileged access, or Critical Infrastructure access.

2. *The Third-Party Vendors*:
Authenticating outside suppliers using their own devices will help reduce the operational costs associated with communicating and resolving login issues. But make sure that they have the proper security protocols installed onto them, that fit in line and accordance with your security policies!

3. *The End Users*:
A frictionless experience to access these services from multiple devices will be of great convenience. For businesses in the B2C space (retail banking, e-commerce, etc.), going passwordless

will help eliminate exposure to stolen customer credential-related breaches. This will allow quick compliance with the data privacy laws of the GDPR, CCPA, HIPAA, and so on.

Set-Up the Plan

Finally, remember that trying to implement a passwordless society must be planned out thoroughly and completely, just like for the Zero Trust Framework and a Privileged Access Management solution. Here is a sample of such a plan:

1. *Define the goals*:
   In this regard, it is very important to understand your vision, business focus, security, privacy, usability, and regulatory requirements, as stated earlier.
2. *Use a platform-based approach*:
   Access management platforms can enable a passwordless society which will allow for flexibility for adoption. These kinds will provide support for FIDO2 and will enhance their product as the protocols and technology evolve.
3. *Go in phases*:
   At this stage, it is important to identify application(s) with the maximum business impact, best suited for the user demographic and technology fit for the passwordless society. Learn and build from the initial success to eventually extend passwordless authentication to the rest of the enterprise land-scape in a gradual approach.
4. *Set realistic goals*:
   Moving to passwordless authentication is not just a technology change, but also a mindset shift. Start with enabling passwordless as an MFA, for desktop login, while keeping an option for users to continue with passwords, and phasing them out as adoption grows and matures.
5. *Focus on end-user training*:
   Most importantly, end-user acceptance and adoption of passwordless authentication is critical for the success of going into a passwordless society. Thus, it is very important to take whatever time is needed to build user awareness and rollout guidelines to enable adoption.

6. *Establish metrics*:

Here, seek end-user feedback and review challenges and learning to bring improvements. Build metrics and Key Performance Indicators (KPIs). A good example of one is to measure the percentage of password use per application and the number of passwordless registrations/logins.

These steps are diagrammed in Figure 4.1.

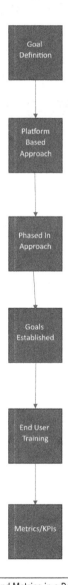

Figure 4.1   The Establishment of KPIs and Metrics in a Privileged Access Management (PAM) Model.

In conclusion, Figure 4.2 shows an image of what a Passwordless Society would theoretically look like.

Figure 4.2   The Passwordless Society.

Index

Note: Page numbers in *italics* indicate figures, and page numbers in **bold** indicate tables in the text

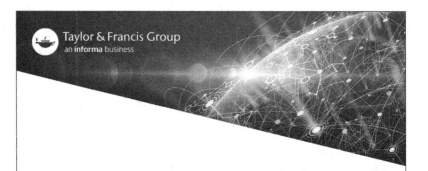

Printed in the United States
by Baker & Taylor Publisher Services